J.H Worcester

The power and weakness of money

J.H Worcester

The power and weakness of money

ISBN/EAN: 9783743463530

Manufactured in Europe, USA, Canada, Australia, Japa

Cover: Foto ©Suzi / pixelio.de

Manufactured and distributed by brebook publishing software (www.brebook.com)

J.H Worcester

The power and weakness of money

THE

POWER AND WEAKNESS

OF

MONEY.

BY

J. H. WORCESTER, Jr., D. D.,

Pastor of the Sixth Presbyterian Church of Chicago.

PHILADELPHIA:
PRESBYTERIAN BOARD OF PUBLICATION
AND SABBATH-SCHOOL WORK,
No. 1334 Chestnut Street.

CONTENTS.

I.
THE POWER AND WEAKNESS OF MONEY . . . . . PAGE 5

II.
THE PERILS OF MONEY-GETTING 23

III.
THE HASTE TO BE RICH 41

IV.
THE CHRISTIAN LAW OF TRADE 63

V.
COVETOUSNESS AND RETRIBUTION 83

VI.
MONEY AS A TEST OF CHARACTER 107

I.

THE POWER AND WEAKNESS OF MONEY.

I.

The Power and Weakness of Money.

AS I waited for a train one day in a railway-station I heard two men conversing in a rather irreverent and bantering way about religion. "Yes," said one, whose dress bespoke him a laboring-man not overburdened with this world's goods, "I believe in religion. Money! That's my religion. That does about everything for a man, as near as I can find out." Ah! thought I; your jest is more than half earnest. Nor are you alone in devotion to the religion you so frankly profess. There are thousands and tens of thousands of your fellow-citizens who deep down in their hearts cherish the same unspoken creed and live up to it with unswerving, and even passionate, devotion. Jesus recognized the existence of such a religion and its popularity in his day when he spoke of mammon as God's great rival for the homage and service of mankind. There has been no age in which mammon has wanted worshipers, but it may be doubted if there ever was an age of which this worship was more characteristic than our own. Each age has its peculiar stamp, and it has been justly said that, as there have been ages of military conquest, ages of religious enthusiasm, ages of intellectual activity and productiveness, ages of political ferment and struggle, so ours is peculiarly a commercial, money-getting and money-loving age. Indeed, I am inclined to think that the power of money is actually greater in this age than it has ever been before. I do not mean that the purchasing power of a given sum is greater, but that the range of its resources is wider. The growth of civilization and the enlargement of the means of communication have added to the variety of the things which money can purchase and brought them more fully within reach, while, at the same time, the safeguards of constitutional government render the tenure of wealth more secure and its employment in large enterprises safer and more profitable.

This feature of the age is intensified in a nation like our own, which is still largely absorbed in the development of material resources the almost boundless extent of which dazzles and bewitches us. In such an age and such a nation there is special occasion for the careful study, in its relation to the Christian life, of the whole subject of MONEY.

It will be observed that that candid mammon-worshiper of mine was ready to give a reason for the faith that was in him. Money was his religion because it would do pretty much everything for a man, as near as he could find out. Not a bad reason, if true. That which can do everything for a man—supply all his wants, shield him from all perils, extricate him from all difficulties and satisfy all his cravings, and that for ever—does he not well to make it his god? Beyond question it is such a belief in the practically unlimited power of money—a conviction that it will do for men, if not absolutely all they care for, at least all that they care most for—which leads them to pursue it with such an eager and consuming passion. "Ah!" cries the youth; "money is the true Aladdin's lamp which brings everything to one's feet. A golden key opens all doors. Give me but money, and I can then indulge my appetites, gratify my tastes, carry out my projects, realize my ambitions, foil my enemies, command the homage of the multitude." So he surrenders his whole time and all his powers to this one pursuit with an intensity, with an absorption, which will never be tempered till his eyes are opened to a sober estimate of the power, to a clear perception of the weakness, of money.

Money is power; there can be no question of that. The Scriptures are full of warnings against the love of money and the peril of riches, but they nowhere deny—on the contrary, they frankly assert—the power of money. "The rich man's wealth is his strong city. The destruction of the poor is their poverty;"* "The poor is hated even of his own neighbor; but the rich hath many friends;" † "A feast is made for laughter, and wine maketh merry; but money answereth all things." ‡ Such, right or wrong, are the facts. Nor do the Scriptures denounce money itself as an evil. The *love* of money is a root of all kinds of evil, but riches are among the rewards promised to the upright. Divine wisdom holds length of days in her right hand; in her left hand, riches and honor. In truth, the power to make and to use money is one of the marks of man's superiority to the beasts that perish, and lies at the foundation of all progress in civilization.

Money, or wealth (for it is in this broad sense that the word is here used), is simply the accumulated product of labor in an exchangeable form. The brute does not accumulate. The squirrel, to be sure, lays in his store of nuts for winter; but he consumes it all, and finds himself in the spring just where he was a year ago. But man takes in the chase or reaps from the field twice what he needs for his own use, and then exchanges his surplus product for that of his neighbor.

* Prov. x. 15. † Prov. xiv. 20. ‡ Eccl. x. 19.

And as this accumulated product multiplies and barter increases, wants enlarge, taste develops and thought expands with leisure, higher aspirations are born, the tent gives place to the city, and the complex fabric of civilized society begins to rise. And he who has this accumulated product in a form which others desire, has the power to command their services, and so far forth to multiply himself, to become two men or three or a thousand.

Thus money lengthens man's arm till it reaches across the sea, and strengthens it till it bores through mountains, yokes the steam to his cars and sends the lightning on his errands. Money is the power by which man converts his thoughts into reality. Columbus may guess at a new world, but only Isabella's jewels can enable him to find it. Michael Angelo may dream a magnificent temple, but it will take the pope's treasures to transmute that dream into stone. Morse may invent an electric telegraph, but it will require the aid of the nation's treasury to stretch its wires between two cities. It is this—not its power to minister to indulgence, but its power to promote achievement—which gives to wealth its chief value in the eyes of the more high-minded of its pursuers.

In fine, money commands indefinitely the resources of the material world.

Then this power has a constant tendency to increase.

"Unto every one that hath shall be given."* A fortune grows like a rolling snow-ball. He who starts in life with only his two hands must toil harder for his first hundred of savings than for his next thousand. In this sense, certainly, "the rich man's wealth is his strong city."† Capital gives its possessor an advantage at every turn: it enables him to attempt larger ventures, to tide over his losses, to wait for his gains, to bear down competition.

This is the legitimate power of wealth—a power which would be inseparable from it even in an unfallen world dealing, as ours does, with material things. But, besides all this, in a fallen world like this—a world in which men are willing to betray their convictions and barter the approval of their conscience for the gratification of their lusts and passions—money confers another and a terrible power. It enables its possessor to purchase, in a certain sense, the souls of men as well as their goods and their muscle. It blinds men's judgment; it buys their votes; it perverts justice; it surrounds its possessor with a host of servile flatterers eager to minister to his vanity and to pander to his vices; it lifts him into a conspicuousness to which his merits give him no claim, gives him an influence utterly out of proportion to his ability, and shields him too often, as in a fort-

* Matt. xxv. 29. † Prov. x. 15.

ress, from the consequences of his crimes. Ignorance, stupidity, vulgarity, selfishness, depravity,—money enough will cover them all. No matter how hideous the image, if it be gilded society will set it upon a pedestal and fall down and worship it.

Is it any wonder that the young man looking on this spectacle, as he may see it any day enacted before his eyes, should exclaim, "Yes, money is all-powerful. Oh, Mammon, be thou my god! Give me but these things—luxury, splendor, power of achievement, immunity, adulation, influence—and I will fall down and worship thee"?

Yet the young man, before he concludes this bargain, will do well to pause long enough to look at the other side. He should make at least a partial inventory of the things that money cannot procure. Simon the magician seems to have been one of those who acted on this theory of the omnipotence of money. In the life, half of charlatan, half of dupe, which he had led before Peter met him, he had found, like enough, that money answered all things. He had nothing that he would not sell for money, and he had wanted nothing that he could not buy for money. And when he saw a new power that he did not possess, when he saw the manifestation of the Holy Ghost in miraculous gifts, tongues, prophecies, gifts of healing, following the laying on of Peter's hands, he came to him, nothing doubting, and offered him money, saying, "Give me also this power, that on whomsoever I lay hands he may receive the Holy Ghost." With an indignant scorn, swift but not unjust, Peter replied, "Thy money perish with thee, because thou hast thought that the gift of God may be purchased with money."* The pith and the sting of this reply lay in these words, "the gift of God." The case so stated needed no arguing. Simon's mistake was in supposing that the Holy Ghost was Peter's gift. Had it been, there had at least been a chance that it was purchasable. Money may prevail for man with man; it cannot prevail for man with God. What should the Sovereign of the universe have to do with a price or a bribe?

Here is his fatal oversight who talks of the omnipotence of money. The power of money is no greater than the power of man. The whole power of money lies in the fact that it represents what other men want, and is therefore an inducement to them to serve us. What is in the power of man's will to grant is within the possibilities of money to purchase. But it so happens that the best things in life are not in the power of man's will at all. The highest of them are gifts of God alone, and even those which are the gifts of man are not in the control of his will, will not pass

* Acts viii. 19, 20.

at his bidding, and hence cannot be matter of bargain and sale. Take, for example, the human affections. They are more precious than gold; life is nothing without them; and yet all the gold of California could not buy so much as one grain of them.

"The rich hath many friends."* Yes, such as they are. Doubtless, if sycophants be friends, if leeches be friends. But let him lose his wealth, and he will not be long in finding that of true friends—friends not to his purse, but to him—among all these he had just so many, and no more, as his own true worth could win.

The millionaire may easily buy a wife—*i. e.*, he need not go far to find a woman who for the bribe of luxury, of show, of social position will go to the altar with him and take the solemn vow, "Until death us do part." But, though he may buy her hand with these things, he cannot buy her heart. Even though she pledge it and mean to sell it, she will find that she can never deliver it. Hearts are not merchandise. A pure love must be given freely or not at all. Nay, the rich man, if he longs for that treasure, may often wish himself poor—at least, for a day—that so he might be sure that what he has won is a true affection, and not the base counterfeit that cleaves only to his purse.

* Prov. xiv. 20.

The old miser may receive on his dying bed the assiduous attentions of children who hope to divide his inheritance; yet all the millions he can leave them will not purchase so much as one spark of sincere affection or one tear of genuine filial sorrow to fall upon his coffin.

Even the respect of one's fellow-men is more than money can buy. It can buy flattery; it can buy servility; it can buy a certain sort of awe of its power. But, unless back of the well-filled purse there be a manhood which riches cannot augment nor the loss of them diminish, men will despise even while they fawn. So money may buy votes, but it cannot buy convictions. It may bring troops of hired advocates to defend a cause or troops of mercenary soldiers to fight for it; but the advocates will lack the power which goes with sincerity, the soldiers the courage born of devotion. Alas for the man, be he rich as Solomon himself, who has won even from his fellow-men only that which is within their power to sell, and therefore within the power of his money to buy!

If, then, the best gifts even of men cannot be purchased with money, how much less the gifts of God!

Even the lowest of these—bodily health—is beyond the power of money to purchase. Money may sometimes do a great deal for the sick. It secures travel, change of air and scene, the highest medical and surgical skill, and so repairs what else might have been past saving; yet at the most far-famed health-resorts of Europe, surrounded with the costliest appointments, ministered to by the most skillful physicians, you may find men and women who would give gold and jewels, houses and lands, almost without stint, for the health of the poorest day-laborer that passes beneath their windows. But they cannot get it. The gift of God cannot be purchased with money.

Just as little are intellectual gifts within the power of money. To one who has these gifts money is often a boon. It secures opportunities for their culture and exercise which otherwise were beyond his reach. But all the money in the world cannot buy the gifts themselves. The vulgar *parvenu* may fill his gallery with the costliest pictures, but he cannot buy the artist's eye to enjoy them, still less the artist's hand to paint that which shall be worthy to hang by their side. If, with the youthful Milton, one burns with the high longing to "leave something so writ to after-times as that they shall not willingly let it die," money will not help him beyond what he needs for his daily bread. The power to write thus is the gift of God. He who has it in him will reveal it though he be as poor as Bunyan; he who has it not cannot buy it though he be as rich as Rothschild.

Far more needful than either of these, but quite as

much beyond buying, is peace of conscience. Judas tried that purchase once, but he found that the thirty pieces of silver for which he had so lightly sold his integrity could not buy back his peace. Take to heart the lesson, you who are bartering honor and manhood to-day for the riches you consider so all-sufficient. Human judges you may bribe, but the Judge who sits on that inner tribunal—never! If you would know how little riches will comfort you when once he arouses himself and thunders forth his condemning sentence, go look at Charles IX. dying in the agonies of remorse amid the splendors of a throne.

"Deep are the wounds which sin has made;
Where shall the sinner find a cure?"

There *is* a cure even for a wounded conscience—a cure by which even the torture of remorse can be stilled for ever in a peace which passeth understanding; but it is the gift of God, offered to the richest as to the poorest, "without money and without price,"* at the cross of Christ.

Nor yet can graces of character, beauty of soul, be purchased with money. Riches may, indeed, be so used as to be a discipline of character, but so may poverty. So far as that goes, all conditions are alike to one who will use them rightly. But to be rich

* Isa. lv. 1.

will not make us one whit more loving or gentle or lowly or brave or true or pure, not one whit more like Christ. These are the treasures of the soul, but they cannot be exchanged for treasure at one's banker's. They are the gift of God. In their genuine perfection they are "the fruit of the Spirit,"* found oftenest, and in greatest loveliness perhaps, with "the poor of this world, rich in faith, and heirs of the kingdom which God hath promised to them that love him." †

Then when, at last, the "successful" career has been run to the end, when the fortune has been amassed, the luxury enjoyed, the things that are for sale bought and consumed, when the shadows begin to gather and the inexorable messenger is heard knocking at the door, money will buy no respite from his summons. Life is a gift of God, and riches will buy no lengthening of its span. "They that trust in their wealth and boast themselves in the multitude of their riches, none of them can by any means redeem his brother nor give to God a ransom for him (for the redemption of their soul is precious, and it ceaseth for ever), that he should still live for ever, and not see corruption." ‡ All the millions of a Vanderbilt cannot add one hour to his life, as he lies there heavily breathing in the stupor of apoplexy. A man of vast wealth was once told by his medical attendant, a London physician of

* Gal. v. 22.   † James ii. 5.   ‡ Ps. xlix. 6-9.

great celebrity, that he had but a few hours to live. "Sir," said he, "I am worth such a sum, and I will give you so many hundred pounds if you will prolong my life till such a time, that I may finish certain important business." The physician shook his head. "I have remedies to sell," was his reply, "but *no time.*" No; time is God's, and he does not sell it. To me there is no more striking exhibition of the weakness of money than in this simple fact—that, with all its power to buy the good things of this world, it cannot buy us so much as one hour in which to enjoy them.

If in the hour of death money be powerless to help, how much less can it avail at the gate of heaven! Has it ever happened to you, my reader, to find yourself without a penny in your pocket in a strange city, where there was no one whom you knew to identify you that you might secure a little credit? If it has, however large your bank-account might be, you found yourself for the time being no better than a pauper. You knew—for a few minutes at least—how it feels to be penniless. If even when your money was in one city and you in another it could do you so little good, how will it be when your money is in one world and you in another? It must be a strange sensation for the man who for years has been wont to buy his way everywhere, to whom it has been but a flourish of the pen and his most extravagant wish was gratified, who has been accustomed to unvarying deference from all whom he met, to find himself at last, stripped of the only power he has ever trusted in or learned to use, standing before that incorruptible tribunal where rich and poor meet together, pleading, "Lord, Lord, open unto me," only to hear the reply, "I know you not."* "The gift of God is eternal life through Jesus Christ our Lord;" † and that gift is free. The whole world will not buy it. The dying thief upon the cross, whose very garments are now the spoil of the soldiers who crucified him, can have it for nothing.

So little, after all, is the boasted power of money. So great within a certain sphere as to seem almost omnipotent, that sphere, the moment we begin to measure it, amazes us by its narrowness. Outward it reaches no farther than to the few poor things men have to sell: it does not touch their convictions, their conscience, nor their heart. Upward it stops short altogether of the intellectual and the spiritual, and forward it reaches no farther than the grave. If of such a power, so limited, you who read these pages can still deliberately say that it will content you, you have already parted with your birthright as an immortal being made in God's image, and have gone down to grovel with the beasts of the field.

* Matt. xxv. 11, 12. † Rom. vi. 23.

II.

THE PERILS OF MONEY-GETTING.

II.
The Perils of Money-Getting.

THERE is a caution in the first of Paul's letters to Timothy the precise point of which is perhaps not always recognized by the reader: "They that will be rich fall into temptation and a snare, and into many foolish and hurtful lusts, which drown men in destruction and perdition."*

It is not the rich, it will be observed, of whom this is said, but those that will be—are determined to be—rich. Elsewhere, indeed, there are warnings quite as urgent addressed to those who possess riches; this is for those who pursue them. The pursuit may or may not be successful; that is nothing to the purpose. The words come home with the same force to the struggling clerk or mechanic as to the millionaire. That man makes a sad mistake who takes it for granted that because he is as poor as Lazarus he is as sure of being carried by angels to Abra-

* 1 Tim. vi. 9.

ham's bosom. There is many a poor man whose heart is set on riches; there are at least some rich men whose hearts are not. It is there, in the heart set on riches, that the danger lies. To such a heart, failure, disappointment, but sharpens the temptation.

"Riches" and "poverty," be it remembered, are relative terms. He is rich who has more than his neighbors; he is poor who has less. No man accounts himself rich who is only as well off as the average of the community in which he lives. Neither—which is more to the purpose—do his neighbors account him rich. The desire to be rich is distinctly the desire to have more than others. It is one form of that love of pre-eminence which runs through everything human, from base-ball up to statesmanship. He who says to himself, "I intend to be rich," means, "I intend to have a larger capital, to build a finer house, to drive a costlier equipage, to dress my family in richer fabrics or to adorn my walls with choicer pictures, than my neighbors." And if, when he is able to do all this, he still does not account himself rich, it is because he knows of some one else who can do more. The reason why the man who has a million will tell you, and in all soberness, that he is not a rich man is that he knows of some one who has two hundred millions. It is this feverish restlessness, satisfied with no measure of comfort and competence so long as there are others who have a greater, that is driving thousands to-day to the very brink of ruin, bodily, mental and moral.

Dr. T. S. Hamlin of Washington quotes some one as having said to him "that the word 'million' had done more mischief in America than any other single word. Said he, 'Nobody thinks there is any happiness in life unless he has a million. Persons who have a little more than a competence are stretched up to be millionaires, and therefore moderate expectations are out of fashion, and our young men go laboring on with a million in their minds, which they seldom reach, and therefore are disappointed.'"

In every community you will find those on whom this fever has seized. They have made up their minds to be rich. This is their ambition, this is their plan of life; and such is the power of concentration of purpose that if they bend all their energies to this one thing there is a very good chance that they will succeed. But the chance is also that they will succeed only at the cost of all that makes riches worth having or life worth living.

For he who sets before himself riches as his end in life bases his life on a mistake—the mistake of proposing to himself an end which has in it nothing moral. Riches have no essential relation to character; neither if a man have them is he the better, neither if he have them not is he the worse. He who has them may be anything from a Montefiore to a Tweed. In the pursuit of such an end, therefore, there is nothing that of itself tends to ennoble character or to quicken conscience, to curb selfishness or to enlarge sympathy. But to set the heart on anything apart from character, to fix the eye and concentrate the endeavor upon any goal which can be reached without gain to manhood, is to put character itself in the greatest jeopardy.

Besides, he who determines to be rich makes the mistake of choosing an end which he has no assurance that it is in his power to reach honorably. Wealth, where it is not accidental or hereditary, is simply pre-eminent success in money-making. But pre-eminent success implies pre-eminent faculty. It is no more in every man to be a great merchant or great railroad-man than it is to be a great orator or great general. In fact, the conduct of a large business, the successful management of great capital, require qualities as marked and peculiar in their way as the management of a campaign. I have a sincere respect for the ability and energy of the man who has worked his way up by honorable means from poverty to a fortune. I may not respect the man—that depends on how he uses his fortune after he has acquired it—but I respect profoundly the talent displayed. It is talent of a high order. But just because it is talent of a high order it is something which most do not possess. High talent of any sort is rare, and there may be very high talent in other directions, with none at all in this. One may have a genius for art or philosophy or jurisprudence, with no more faculty for money-making than a child. The simple truth is, the most of us are just average men and women—which is very fortunate for the world. But when an average man sets out to make a colossal fortune, he is under a tremendous temptation to cheat in order to do it. If your horse is not as fast as your competitor's, and yet you are bound to win the race, you will have to lame the other horse or bribe the jockey.

Yet, again, he who says, "I will be rich," sets before himself that which it may be no part of God's plan that he should achieve, even though he have the faculty. Every man's life is a plan of God. He has a certain work for each to do—a certain discipline for each to pass through. Man's only safety, morally and spiritually, lies in finding out that plan and following it. But that plan may not lie in the line of his ambition, nor even in the apparent line of his gifts. There are some who, though they have the ability to gain riches, have not the ability to use them wisely. God sees that they cannot safely be trusted with riches; or the capacities which would make a great financier may in God's plan need to be subordinated to the capacities which will make a great discoverer or a great missionary. He, then, who sets his heart on being rich runs the risk of finding himself involved in a lifelong contest with the providence and the Spirit of God.

What now should a man look for who has set his heart upon something which has in it nothing essentially moral, something which it may not be within his capacity to reach honorably, and something which it may be no part of God's plan that he should reach, but to fall into temptation and a snare, and into many foolish and hurtful lusts which drown men in destruction and perdition?

The choice of a merely material good, the stress laid upon money-power and the class of things which it brings within reach, expose him to the danger of undervaluing the moral as compared with the material all through life. Money is power, but it is power of an inferior sort, outranked by intellectual power, moral power and spiritual power. He who fixes his thought upon it runs the risk of undervaluing all these higher sorts of power in comparison with it. He looks at things from the wrong angle and sees life in a false perspective. He measures things, he measures men, by a wrong standard. The men he worships are not the spiritual heroes and kings of humanity, but the money-kings. Jesus himself, if he stood before him to-day, as he stood before Nicodemus and Simon the Pharisee, in the plain garb of the poor carpenter and itinerant preacher, would hardly attract his notice. The qualities which he most assiduously cultivates in himself are not those which will render him most tenderly loved or most highly serviceable to his fellow-men. On the contrary, some of the noblest qualities will be in imminent danger of repression and atrophy because of their tendency to interfere with rapid accumulation.

But we shall see this more clearly if we look in detail at a few of the perils which this passion for money-getting involves.

Look, then, first, at the grosser forms of temptation which arise from the disproportion between men's desires and their capacity. When a man having set his heart on riches finds out that he has not the ability to command them by the straight though rugged path of industry, what then? Then there present themselves two other paths with much flattering promise of conducting him more swiftly and surely to the desired goal—the path of chance, and the path of deceit.

There is the path of chance. If I cannot earn money, I can gamble for it. A fool has an equal chance with an Astor if both stake their money on a throw of the dice. And so the lottery, the gaming-table, the exchange, are crowded with a throng who, not content with the moderate competence which their industry might earn, are struggling with insane eagerness to get something for nothing.

On the other side, there is the path of deceit and fraud. What but this thirst for riches, this restless discontent with modest profits and a frugal support, this relentless competition of all for the glittering prizes which only a few can attain, is responsible for the thousand forms of petty fraud with which, business-men themselves being witnesses, the commercial world is honeycombed? It is a common thing for pastors to hear from members of their flock such expressions as these: "In my business it is impossible to live up to an ideal standard of honesty and make money;" "I am compelled by the stress of competition to do things in my business from which my conscience recoils." A Christian merchant, for instance, in a thoroughly reputable and substantial line of business once assured me that in his business it was impossible to make money if goods were represented to customers as they really are. "Such is the demand for cheap goods," he said, in substance, "that manufacturers find themselves compelled to do cheap, flimsy work, which by a little extra finish may be made to look well when new, but which will not wear. Yet it will not do for me to offer this as second-class work; otherwise, my customer will betake himself forthwith to my competitor over the way, who will show him the same goods at the same price with the unblushing assurance that it is a first-class article, and he will buy of him." Professor Phelps of Andover, quotes a shrewd observer as saying, "The ways of trade have become selfish to the borders of theft, and supple to the borders of fraud;" and also, in allusion to the oaths of the custom-house, "We eat and drink and wear perjury in a hundred commodities." It would be easy to multiply such expressions with reference to many different kinds of business. It would be easy to name more than one instance of a conscientious young man leaving the service of a professedly Christian employer because, according to his own statement, he could not do what was required of him without what he regarded as dishonesty. Such representations must pass for what they are worth—I am quite willing to believe that there is exaggeration in them—but they show how a host of men feel. And when men feeling so are bent upon being rich, it is easy to guess how they are likely to set about it. The truth, perhaps, is about this—that in most lines of business a man with great sagacity and skill can make a fortune, and a man of average ability a living and something over, by methods of strict Christian integrity. But the average man is not content with that. Moderate success does not satisfy him; he wants to be rich. So what God denies him he consents to seek from the devil.

Here might be included also the snare of evil companionships and entangling alliances. From estimating men by the money-standard it is but a step to choosing associates by that standard. I should not be drawing on my imagination were I to tell of a Christian merchant deliberately forming a partnership with one whose business methods he had long known to be without honor or scruple, because the alliance held out a prospect of increased profits.

But suppose that a high sense of honor, an incorruptible integrity, is proof against these grosser temptations, or that commanding ability in some measure lifts one above them; does that make the pursuit of riches safe? Far from it. There are subtler snares which are so much the more dangerous in that they are less palpable. There is, for example, the snare of covetousness. At the start, perhaps, the young man does not seek money for its own sake. He is a young man of generous impulses, who sincerely loves to help others, and he has rose-colored visions of what he will do with his wealth when it is won. He had, it may be, some struggles with himself over the question whether he ought to enter a money-making career rather than one poorer in earthly rewards, but richer in opportunities of usefulness. But he has quieted these misgivings by the promises he has made to himself respecting the use of his gains. As he has gone on, however, the sense of possession has grown sweeter and sweeter to him. The reproductive power of capital has laid hold of his imagination, till finally the great worth of money in his eyes has come to be, not its power to relieve distress, to enlighten ignorance, to promote science, to spread the gospel, but its power to gain more money. Every dollar that he gives away costs him a pang because he seems to himself to be not giving an apple, but cutting down a tree; in other words, to be parting not merely with the dollar that he holds in his fingers, but with all the other dollars which that one would have produced at compound interest during the remainder of his life. Hence the phenomenon, so sadly common as to seem almost the rule, of the spirit of liberality waning as the means of liberality increase—the phenomenon so aptly expressed by the rich man who said, "When I had a shilling hand, I had a guinea heart; but now that I have guinea hand, I have but a shilling heart."

Here, too, we must take note of the temptation to moral cowardice which attends the desire of riches. It is no slander upon the rich to say that they are seldom the leaders of any great moral reform: the pocket-nerve is too sensitive. The same is true of those who are bent on being rich. Money, we say, is conservative. It is so in a good sense. There is no better cure for communism and anarchism than a homestead or a deposit in a savings-bank. It is so in a bad sense also. It makes men timid. It muzzles them. It makes them shy of the unpopular side. It puts a cold worldly wisdom in the place of enthusiasm. Robert Hall was once arguing with a clergyman who was suspected of having changed his opinions from mercenary motives. Proposing to him several reforms of great importance, Mr. Hall was invariably met with the reply, "I don't see it," "I can't see it at all." At length, penciling in small letters the word "God" upon an envelope which lay upon the table, Mr. Hall showed it and asked: "Can you see that?"—"Yes." Then, covering it with a half sovereign, he asked again, "Can you see it now?"—"No." Whereupon without another word he went away.

Finally, most insidious of all, most rarely escaped by those who will be rich, is the snare of worldliness—insidious because worldliness is so intangible a thing. You cannot analyze it into separate acts; you cannot pierce it with an express "Thou shalt not." You cannot bring a bill of indictment against it in definite courts and convict men of it as you may of lying or profanity. It hangs about men like an impure atmosphere, of which those are least sensible who have breathed it longest. True, there are few paths in life which lead clear of this snare. The danger of losing sight, in our preoccupation with the seen and temporal, of the unseen and eternal besets us on every hand. Still, there is a great difference in the degree in which different pursuits tend to unfit the mind for spiritual exercises, and hardly one seems so antagonistic to them as an eager pursuit of wealth. Those who will be rich find the thought of money pursuing them everywhere. The columns of a ledger project themselves upon the pages of their open Bibles; calculations of profit and loss pursue them to their closets, and they plan their next week's ventures even in the house of God. That such cares leave so little time for what is spiritual is not so bad as that they leave so little heart for it. It was this benumbing spiritual influence against which the Master himself uttered so clear a warning in his parable of the Sower: "He also that received seed among the thorns is he that heareth the word; and the care of this world, and the deceitfulness of riches, choke the word, and he becometh unfruitful."*

Such warnings of Christ and his apostles are not out of date now, as some men seem to think. Human nature has not changed with the progress of the centuries. The love of money lies as deep in men's

* Matt. xiii. 22.

hearts and is as fruitful a root of evil in this nineteenth century as in the first. All over our land to-day the frosts of worldliness have touched the Church and chilled its zeal, checked its fruit-bearing and sealed up the streams of its beneficence. And when we search for the cause, we find it here in the mad chase after riches, of this trading, money-loving age. Samson is falling asleep in the lap of the Delilah of prosperity. The watchmen all along the walls of Zion may be heard sounding out from one to another the note of warning. Ministers when they meet, earnest Christians in the prayer-meeting and the convention, ask each other, "What can be done to stay this tide of worldliness that is coming in upon us like a flood?" And they see no hope in anything save a financial crash like that which was followed by such blessed spiritual results at the East in 1857.

Well, what then? Are all to turn away from money-making as from a thing irreconcilable with Christian living? Impossible! That were to thwart the plan of Providence and bring the world to a standstill. Money-making is perilous business. He who thinks otherwise is already caught in the snare. Yet it does not follow that men should not brave its perils if God calls them to do it. It does follow that they should not brave them for the mere excitement of the pursuit or for the mere luxuries which wealth can procure. The difference between heroism and foolhardiness is a difference of motive. Safety is not the only thing to be considered in choosing one's calling in life. There is heroism in facing moral as well as in facing physical perils if the motive be worthy. But there is no heroism, there is no wisdom, there is only reckless folly, in ignoring the perils. The money-making life is not, as young men are so apt to esteem it, the most desirable life. Commercial success is not the highest kind of success. The richest men are not, as a rule, the happiest men. Nor are they ordinarily the most spiritual men. I would no more dissuade one from the pursuit of money—ay, of riches, if, on a careful review of the whole situation, he is convinced that in that pursuit he can do most for God and for his fellow-men—than I would dissuade a physician from exposing himself to the small-pox to save life. But I would adjure the physician to vaccinate himself first; and I would commend to the money-getter a like precaution. Is it asked, "How shall this be done?" In three ways. First, by a consecrated purpose—by penetrating the soul through and through with the conviction that the one thing needful is not money, that its value is solely as a means to an end, and that that end, to be kept in view as steadily in the counting-room as in the closet, is to be the kingdom of God and his righteousness. Secondly, by a consciousness of stewardship—by remembering that in all our business we are simply the agents for a divine Principal, and that all our gains must be accounted for to the Owner. Thirdly, by the cultivation of a contented spirit—the spirit that knows both how to be full and to be hungry, both how to abound and to suffer need; the spirit that, having food and raiment can be therewith content, *because* it has found in the true riches a satisfaction so real and abiding that it can accept without chafing or impatience whatever limit of earthly prosperity God pleases to set. There is wisdom in that old prayer of Agur, so foreign to the spirit of our age that one sometimes wonders whether any one ever prays it now: "Give me neither poverty nor riches; feed me with food convenient for me; lest I be full, and deny thee, and say, Who is the Lord? or lest I be poor, and steal, and take the name of my God in vain." There is both peace and safety in the spirit that can sing with Bunyan's shepherd-boy:

> "Content am I with what I have,
>   Little be it or much;
> And, Lord, contentment still I crave,
>   Because thou savest such.

> "Fullness to such a burden is
>   As go on pilgrimage;
> Here little, and hereafter bliss,
>   Is best from age to age."

III.

THE HASTE TO BE RICH.

III.

The Haste to be Rich.

WHEN an epidemic breaks out in a community, bringing terror and death to numberless homes, the community naturally looks to its physicians to discover and reveal the sources of the contagion that is spreading such havoc, that so the evil may be attacked at its fountain-head, and not only resisted in its progress, but altogether done away. In like manner, when a moral epidemic breaks out, by which character after character is blighted, home after home desolated with a sorrow more bitter than death, the community has a right to look to its soul-physicians for light as to the sources of this moral contagion, that here, too, remedies may be applied which shall arrest the evil by removing its cause.

Such an epidemic is now upon us—an epidemic of dishonesty, of defalcation, of betrayal of trusts. In many cases the criminals are men of high standing in their respective communities, and of eminent business ability, who, by years of laborious devotion to duty, had won for themselves elevated and responsible position and a spotless name, sometimes even had become leaders in the Church. Thus it goes on month after month and year after year, till men's hearts are sick, their faith in man almost destroyed, and their very faith in God tottering. True, no age and no clime is without its wrecks of this sort, as none is without its fevers and its pestilences. What startles us and suggests a search for some new and deep-seated cause is the increasing frequency and magnitude of these moral catastrophes, the unexpected quarters in which they appear, and the high characters and spotless reputations which they involve. Such a cause is not difficult to find. It is suggested in the words of that unsurpassed collection of sound business maxims, the Proverbs of Solomon: "He that maketh haste to be rich shall not be innocent."* The yellow fever is not more distinctly traceable to the uncleaned streets and reeking vaults of Southern cities than is this epidemic of financial crimes to *the haste to be rich.*

In the last chapter were considered the perils of money-getting in general. But there are other and peculiar perils involved in the *haste* to be rich. Here we have the love of money in the most aggravated form, and hence leading to the most disastrous results.

* Prov. xxviii. 20.

Money represents the product of labor. More strictly, it is the product of the exchange of our own labor for that of others. In other words, it is the legitimate reward of service rendered to others with muscle or brain or by the use of that which is one's own. The great value to mankind of the love of money, the offset to the terrible evils which grow out of it, is its efficacy as a spur to useful industry. Without this spur, idleness, a still more fruitful parent of crime than covetousness, would desolate society with ravages that nothing could stay. And so, on the other hand, the great safeguard against the perils of the money-getting spirit is the love of work for its own sake, the desire to be of service to others. Just as a fiery and impatient horse may be made safe and serviceable if harnessed with one of different mettle, patient, strong, and steady, so the love of gain, which, left to itself, rushes headlong with men over precipices to swift destruction, may be made safe and beneficent if firmly yoked with the desire of service. Since, then, money is the legitimate reward of service, the legitimate and honorable way to seek it is by service—in other words, by earning it. It may, indeed, sometimes be honestly come by in other ways. It may be gotten by inheritance or by gift. It may be stumbled upon by some lucky accident of discovery. But we hold in small esteem the man who forsakes the paths of useful industry to *seek* wealth by these methods. The sycophant who dances attendance upon some rich man in the hope of being made his beneficiary or his heir, the Micawber who sits complacently waiting for something to turn up, the laborer who, spade on shoulder, turns from his half-tilled field to dig here, there and everywhere for the buried treasure of some Captain Kidd, are characters whom self-respecting men regard with a sort of pitying contempt. The legitimate way to seek riches is by earning them. So won, a fortune is a reward of merit, the enjoyment of which is enhanced by the consciousness that society has been the gainer for every dollar of which it is made up.

But that road to wealth, like the road to knowledge, is slow and toilsome. A fortune so won represents—and this is just the honor of it—the labor of many years. Here and there transcendent abilities may enable one to render some service to others of such extraordinary value that it shall land him, almost at a bound, in well-earned affluence. But such instances are so rare as not to be worth the seeking. Little by little, step by step—is the law of true progress, the condition, broadly speaking, of all worthy success. But ours is an impatient age. Slow progress does not satisfy it. Men are on the *qui vive* for a short cut to every goal which they seek. The problem of half the world to-day is how to begin at the end; to grasp results without processes, to master sciences without application, trades without apprenticeship, to leap into professional life without a liberal education, into authorship without practice, into office without experience—ay, even to find some "Celestial Railroad" to take them, if not to heaven, at least to the land of Beulah, without the weary plodding up hill and down of the old-fashioned pilgrim. What wonder that, when there is such hurry and impatience everywhere, when the fever to fly rather than to climb so burns in men's bones, they should be in haste to be rich, and should bend all their wits to the solution of the problem how to grasp the rewards of industry without the cost of patient toil. Go to the typical young American of twenty, tell him that if he is diligent, frugal, upright, prudent, he may fairly hope to be a rich man at fifty: will he be satisfied? Not he! He would be rich at twenty-five.

But now take notice that the short cuts in life are always deceitful. They cost more than they come to. There is nothing gained by attempting to gather life's harvests before they are ripe. And if this is true of all short cuts, it is doubly true of the short cut to fortune. If there is anything in the world to which the adage *Slow and sure* emphatically applies, it is to the pursuit of riches. The more brilliant the prize, the greater the hazard. The more sudden the gain, the more chances of failure. Mining, for instance, holds out a promise, to one who strikes a paying claim, of a fortune almost in a day, and yet, of the thousands who, lured on by that promise, tramp up and down the Rocky Mountains and the Sierras digging and prospecting, few make any money, fewer grow rich, fewer still keep their riches till they die. For this is another peculiarity of sudden wealth—that, as it comes, so, as a rule, it goes. The fortune which flies in at one window flies out at another. When riches come suddenly, they do not bring with them the discipline and the experience necessary to keep them. They come into hands too weak and unskillful to hold them, and it is not long before they slip through. Indeed, not only does sudden wealth bring with it no preparation for its reception: it brings, on the contrary, an intoxication which is apt to turn the coolest head and convert the frugal and industrious workman forthwith into a reckless spendthrift or adventurer. Many sudden and brilliant fortunes were made by manufacturers, contractors, and others, during our civil war. Yet only five years later the New York *Nation* remarked:

"The accounts from all the leading markets agree in this—that the fortunes made, the small and large sums gained, during the years of the war, were almost all lost again before the close of 1867."

So little gain is there money-wise in the haste to be rich. In truth, if one strives to get rich by some shorter road than that of patient industry and frugal saving, the chances are very many to one that he will die poor.

But this money-loss is the least part of the evil of such haste to be rich: far more to be dreaded is the damage to character. Let us look into the matter a little and see if this is not true. Our typical young American who would be rich at twenty-five must, of course, find some way of getting money without earning it; for clearly it is not in his power, unless he be a very prodigy, to render to society within that time in substantial services the equivalent of a fortune. Well, such a way is not hard to find. The pickpocket can tell him of one; the forger, of another; the counterfeiter, of another. But these are out of the question: the young man is not a thief.

Well, then, the sporting-man will tell him of another way. He will take him out to the races and give him a "tip" or two by which he may be sure of *winning* as much in a day as he can *earn* in six months. No stealing about that; 'tis an agreement between gentlemen. The loser will pay over his stake with a smile and a bow, and wait till his turn comes to win Or he can buy a ticket in a lottery and stand a chance of getting back a thousand dollars for his ten. Or he can try a quiet little game of faro, and on his meagre clerk's salary can soon manage to drink champagne and drive a fast horse. Suppose he does; is there any sin in it? Is it true that he who in this way makes haste to be rich shall not be innocent?

Fortunately, it is not necessary at this day to stay long upon that question. An enlightened Christian community has pretty well made up its mind as to the sin of gambling in all its forms. The plea on which it is still defended here and there—the plea on which civilized governments, and even churches, sometimes justify a resort to it for revenue—is that of mutual consent. This is what distinguishes it from robbery pure and simple. But it distinguishes it only as it distinguishes dueling from murder, and is as fallacious a defence in the one case as in the other. For that consent is never given in the expectation of a loss; it is the uncertainty, the element of chance, upon which the consent is founded. He who stakes his money on a hazard of any sort does so because he is willing to risk the loss of what is his own for the hope of gaining what is another's. And that which condemns it is the utter absence of that element of mutual benefit, of an equivalent given for service rendered, which is the very essence of trade and industrial pursuits of any kind. It is an effort to obtain something for nothing, and that at another's expense. It cannot be reconciled, therefore, as the laborer's pursuit of wages, the merchant's pursuit of profit, can be, and should be, with the love of service, the wish to benefit others. It cannot be brought under the law, "Thou shalt love thy neighbor as thyself." Its inspiration is selfishness pure and simple—the selfishness which is eager to profit by another's loss, a selfishness cold, hard, sometimes even diabolical, which can coolly pocket its gains in utter indifference to its victim's ruin and despair.

Were there any doubt about this as a matter of abstract reasoning, that doubt would be set at rest by a moment's glance at its effects. That which invariably deteriorates character just in proportion as men give themselves up to it must have something essentially wrong in it, even if we could not find where that wrong lay. Trade has its temptations many and mighty, yet it may be so pursued as to ennoble character, and even to spiritualize it. Not so with gambling. It unsettles good habits, makes wholesome industry distasteful and wellnigh impossible, fosters a passion which destroys self-control, dries up the sympathies, dulls the conscience, and hurries men on to lying, theft and suicide. At Monaco, the gambler's paradise, the number of suicides every winter is said to be so great that they excite scarce a ripple of interest. And, as to fraud, who expects honesty in a confirmed gambler? Where is the merchant who would keep in his employ a clerk whom he knew to be a gambler? And why not? Because, first of all, he would expect such a clerk to be idle and unprofitable, and because, over and above that, he would expect him to a certainty to gamble with his employer's money when his own gave out.

So much for the gambler's way of making haste to be rich. Selfish and immoral in principle, its natural result is bankruptcy both in purse and in character.

But perhaps our youth is too moral to gamble, and yet too impatient to be rich to wait for the slow accumulation of the profits of industry. There is, then, still another alternative: he can *speculate*. This is the commoner way. Where one man seriously sets himself to make a fortune by gambling, a hundred, it may be, set themselves to make one by speculation. It is the more alluring way, because, while it holds out the same prospect of sudden and unlimited gains, and gains bearing no proportion to any equivalent rendered, it wears much more the aspect of *bona-fide* business and is surrounded with associations much less vulgar and repulsive. Since the war of the rebellion the mania for speculation resulting from the sudden fortunes then made has unquestionably grown upon us as a nation, notwithstanding the temporary check and the severe lessons of the panic of 1873, till it has affected our whole commercial life and ensnared with its fascination the entire rising generation which has grown up under its influence.

What shall we say of it? Have we found here a safe and wholesome way of making haste to be rich? Or is this also evil? I desire to speak plainly on this point, but I desire also to speak justly. I am not unmindful of its difficulties, nor of the danger of rash utterances concerning that with the details of which one is not familiar. Indeed, I am inclined to think that what restrains ministers from speaking oftener and with greater emphasis on this subject is not the fear of giving offence, but the fear of doing injustice. It is not well to be reckless for the sake of seeming fearless. Nevertheless, with all these cautions in mind, I cannot say less than this—that to a large extent speculation does not differ from gambling as to its principles, as to its motives, or as to its results. To a large extent, I say. It would be *easier* to leave out this qualification, and say, once for all, that speculation is simply gambling under another name. But one has only to cast about for a definition of speculation to see that this will not do. Webster defines it as follows:

"Speculation [in commerce] is the act or practice of buying land or goods in the expectation of a rise in price, and of selling them at an advance, as distinguished from regular trade, in which the profit expected is the difference between the retail and wholesale prices, or the difference of price in the place where the goods are purchased and the place to which they are carried to market."

If this be speculation, then it is plain that of speculation in the abstract we can affirm neither good nor bad. It may be as legitimate as any other kind of trade. There is no sin in buying a piece of ground that one does not need for present use, in the expectation that within a given time it can be sold for more than it cost. The seller is not wronged, for he receives a fair price for his land. The buyer may even render a service in relieving him of property which he does not want, and supplying him, instead, with a movable capital which he can use. So, too, it is clear that the speculator in grain or in cotton may render an important service to both producer and consumer by bridging a gap between them, taking the product off the hands of the one and carrying it till wanted by the other.

On the other hand, there is a kind of speculation which, on the testimony of speculators themselves, is nothing more nor less than a bet upon the state of the market at a given time in the future. And the difficulty theoretically, the danger practically, lies in this —that speculation of the one sort passes over into speculation of the other by gradations so insensible that it is scarcely possible to put the finger on a given point and say that just here the gambling, and so the sin, begins.

The two things that combine to give speculation the character of gambling are the element of chance and the absence of any exchange of benefits. Just in proportion as these two elements enter into it does speculation cease to be innocent and become a mischievous depredation upon society. And I fear they enter very largely into the most of it. The more purely uncertain the future price of a thing is, the more unequivocally does speculation in it take on the character of betting. But I am afraid that just this element of uncertainty is what creates the fascination for most speculators. In Wall street, for example, they distinguish between investment stocks and speculative stocks, the former being those which have a substantial and ascertainable value, and so fluctuate little; the latter, those which, because they have no definitely ascertainable value, fluctuate constantly, and can be tossed back and forth with the liveliness of a shuttlecock and the beguiling uncertainty of the ball on the roulette-table. In produce speculation is most lively and eager when there is the greatest uncertainty about the crop, or when sudden disturbing intelligence causes prices to rise and fall most rapidly and dubiously. As to the other element, also—the absence of any exchange of benefits—when two men " settle their differences" at the close of a day's transactions on the Board of Trade, what benefit does he who pays receive in exchange more than he who settles his losses at the close of a day's races?" And when men deliberately engineer a "corner" the result of which, if successful, they know will be to crush their victims as in a vise, strip them of their last dollar, and possibly drive them to suicide, and, having succeeded, calmly enforce the consequences, it may well be asked whether the most stony-hearted faro-banker ever reaches a pitch of more hardened selfishness than this. What semblance, what shadow, of the idea of compensation for service is there left in gains so acquired?

The opinions of ministers on this subject are often made light of on two grounds—that they are without practical knowledge of the subject, and that they judge of it by a superfine standard of morality which cannot be applied to practical life. If there has been a man in this country within the last twenty years against whom neither of these objections would lie, it was the late William H. Vanderbilt; yet before a Senate committee on the subject of corners he condemned most unqualifiedly not only corners, but all that kind of speculation known as "selling short"—which consists in selling what one has not got—objecting to the whole system on the ground, not simply that it deranged commerce, but that it fostered in young men the gambling spirit, encouraged idleness and deprived all business in a measure of its solid and legitimate character.

A further confirmation of this view of the general character of speculation is found in the uneasiness of conscience of so many who engage in it.

A man who was prospering in "selling short" on the Board of Trade once told a friend that his pastor had been preaching against the practice, but that it was none of his business: he knew nothing about it. A little later, when he had lost everything, he came to the same friend and told him that he was going to quit the business, for it was nothing but a process of gambling. Such admissions, in such cirumstances, are so common—in fact, I suspect, so nearly the rule—as to point to some deeper cause than the mere exasperation of defeat. The iron-manufacturer who fails does not suspect something sinful in the smelting of iron. The dry-goods merchant who goes to the wall does not announce his determination to have no more to do with so questionable a business. Granting fully that there is such a thing as legitimate speculation, is it not evident that those who seek a fortune by speculation find it so hard to keep within the limits of the legitimate, find the usefulness of their calling so dubious and its temptations so strong, that conscience keeps up an undertone of protest which, though the excitement of success may drown it for a time, is sure to make itself heard in the first pause of adversity?

Above all, this view of the close affinity of speculation with gambling is confirmed by the identity of their effects. In varying degree, according to the kind of speculation indulged in, speculation produces all the destructive moral effects of gambling. The restlessness, the unwholesome craving for excitement, the distaste for productive industry, the inability to stop at a safe point, the reckless spending and extravagant indulgence, the selfish indifference to the loss and suffering one occasions to others, the fierce passions enkindled, the temptation to use the property of others,—all these attach as visibly to the one as to the other. A single fortunate speculation, like a single lottery-prize, often unsettles the business-habits of a lifetime and converts an industrious citizen into a mere adventurer; while, as to the passions aroused, one may read descriptions of scenes upon the Stock and Produce Exchanges during a day of unusual excitement—of the fierce rage, as of wild beasts ready to fly at one another's throat, the voices hoarse with passion, the look of stony despair or incipient madness—which might have been applied, with hardly the change of a syllable, to portray the scenes in the Casino at Monte Carlo or in a gambling-den at Leadville.

But the curse of this craze for sudden wealth

through speculation lies in the strain which it puts upon honesty. One may be permitted to doubt whether any careful business-man would feel much safer with a clerk whom he knew to be bitten with the speculative mania than with a clerk whom he knew to be a gambler. It is this one thing which more than any other lies at the root of those collapses of character of which we are seeking an account. *The* reason why defalcation and embezzlement are so much more common now than fifty years ago is that speculation is so much more rife. Trace back the history of these crimes as they are reported with dreary monotony month after month, and with rare exceptions it may be summed up in two words—*speculation, peculation.* Men on salaries are out of conceit with the idea of laying up by little and little through a careful living inside their income. Men with a little capital laid by will not look at six per cent. They must all take a few dollars and deposit them with some one as a "margin." If they succeed at first, so much the worse, probably. Then the craze becomes wilder. By and by the margin is gone. Then another goes after it, and then another. The reaction which follows such losses is as intense as the extravagance of hope which preceded it. Equanimity is gone; judgment is unbalanced; conscience is relaxed. The safe is full of trust-funds; they can be borrowed for a time, and nobody will be the wiser. The gambler's infatuation, to expect sure success with each new venture, has taken complete possession. All is sure to be made right next time. So the borrowing goes on, till finally it ceases to be borrowing even in name, and becomes downright stealing—stealing of the meanest, most heartless kind, devouring of widows' houses, stealing of the orphan's portion, stealing of the poor man's savings, stealing from the Lord's treasury; and stealing must be covered by lying, wholesale, deliberate, and the rottenness within be cloaked by a mantle of hypocrisy, till the man stands among his fellows a whited sepulchre which indeed outwardly appears beautiful unto men, but within is full of dead men's bones and of all uncleanness. Then the sepulchre collapses, the noisome stench fills the air, and men turn away with loathing from the ruin of that on which a moment before they were lavishing their praise. And all this because of the insane ambition to make money *fast!* "He that maketh haste to be rich shall not be innocent."

Do you wonder that public teachers should sometimes forget to measure their words—that they should find it hard to balance and qualify and discriminate in warning men against a passion which is literally honeycombing society with such moral rottenness as this? When the line that absolutely divides right from wrong is so hard to find, the only real safety lies in keeping a good way this side of it. Do you wonder that any man in whose eyes a good name is better than great riches, and who stops to ask, "What shall it profit a man if he shall gain the whole world and lose his own soul?"* should implore young men—and old men too, for that matter—to beware of speculation, and should bid them, as John the Baptist bade the soldiers who came to him, "Be content with your wages"?†

So I say to you, my reader, you can take no wiser and safer maxim with you through life than this: *Be content with your wages.* Be satisfied with what you can earn. Throttle, the instant it rears its head, that demoniacal passion, the haste to be rich. Banish the desire to get something for nothing. Keep steadily in view the purpose to render a fair equivalent for what you receive. Let the usefulness of your calling be as near a concern to you as its profitableness. Never unyoke the desire of gain from the desire of service, if you would not have it take the bit in its teeth and leap with you into an abyss of moral ruin whence you will escape, if at all, as one washed ashore from a wreck, the whole freightage of your life's voyage gone out of sight for ever, and nothing left but the plank on which you drifted.

* Mark viii. 36. † Luke iii. 14.

IV.

THE CHRISTIAN LAW OF TRADE.

IV.

The Christian Law of Trade.

WE have already had occasion, in considering the perils of money-getting and the peculiar peril of the haste to be rich, to recognize as one great source of these perils—the root-error out of which spring a whole brood of disastrous moral results—the divorce between the desire of gain and the desire of service; in other words, between self-love and love of one's neighbor. It is worth while to fix our attention more closely, however, upon that great law governing all human relations, "Thou shalt love thy neighbor as thyself,"* in its specific application as the fundamental law of trade.

There is no principle of morals more widely accepted in theory than this. Even the agnostic who excuses himself from any obligation to obey that first and great commandment, "Thou shalt love the Lord thy

* Matt. xxii. 39.

God with all thy heart,"* on the plea that he is not sure whether he has a God worthy of love, discourses in far-fetched phrase, but with the best intentions, of egotism and altruism as the centripetal and centrifugal forces whose perfect balance is to keep the social system in harmonious rotation.

And yet one could hardly have a more striking illustration of the tendency of a beautiful generalization to pass over into a glittering generality altogether remote from practical life than the extent to which it is taken for granted, almost as beyond discussion, that this law has not, and even cannot have, any application to that great sphere of human life in which all of us sometimes, and many of us continually, move—the sphere of trade.

Taken for granted, I say. It is indeed a humiliating necessity which one finds himself under of pausing to insist, before going any farther, that this law does apply to trade as much as to anything else. It is a pitiable consequence of the gambling speculations and other sharp expedients for getting something for nothing, which have continued to pass themselves off as legitimate business, that all business has come to wear, in the eyes of many, the aspect of a predatory pursuit —a sort of licensed piracy, whose cardinal principles are such as, "Diamond cut diamond" and, "Eat or be

* Matt. xxii. 37.

eaten." If trade sustains any relation at all to Christianity in the eyes of such, it is as furnishing a money-basis for religious enterprises. The idea that it may be itself a religious enterprise conducted on Christian principles and from Christian motives, they laugh to scorn as the most naïve of illusions. From this point of view the moving spring of all commercial activity is unadulterated selfishness. Or, as Dr. Bushnell strikingly phrases it in his admirable sermon on "How to be a Christian in Trade,"* "What, they ask, is the very operation of merchandising but a drill exercise in selfishness? And what is the law of price or profit but the law of possibility—viz., to ask the highest price the market will bear, be the cost what it may and the value what it may? What, too, is current price itself but a market graduation settled by the contrary bulling and bearing of two selfishnesses?" Well, if this be true, then trade is *sin* for the same reason that gambling is sin or that highway-robbery is sin. The law "Thou shalt love thy neighbor as thyself" is a broad law; it covers every relation of man with his fellow-man. It makes no exceptions; it abandons no department of life to the sway of self-love alone. It does not read, "Thou shalt love thy neighbor as thyself except when he buys from thee or sells to thee." It cannot make exceptions, for

* *Sermons on Living Subjects*, Sermon XIII.

love makes none. He who truly loves his neighbor loves him everywhere and always—as much when he is bargaining with him as when he is praying with him.

But the whole assumption is false. Trade is not only bound to be brought under this law: it can be brought under it. There is nothing in the idea of legitimate trade which conflicts in any way with the disinterested purpose to benefit one's neighbors. The common notion that there can be but one good side to a bargain is as monstrous as the notion that there can be but one good side to a marriage, the simple truth being that the only honest bargain, as the only worthy marriage, is the one which has two good sides.

The foundation of all trade is simple barter—an exchange of something which I want less and you want more for something which you want less and I want more. Certainly there are two good sides to such an exchange. If Cain and Abel exchanged, the one some of his corn for some of the other's sheep, both were the better off if the exchange was fair. And when a medium of exchange is contrived, portable, durable, easily subdivided and estimated, and called "money," that in nowise alters the essential nature of the transaction or lessens this feature of mutual advantage. Society advances by division of labor. While each is his own farmer and herdsman and butcher and tailor and shoemaker and carpenter and blacksmith and mason, civilization cannot rise beyond its most rudimentary stage; but the farther the division of labor is carried, the more indispensable and complex becomes the exchange of products which we call "trade." And as this process broadens and grows more complicated the whole vast fabric of producers, carriers, manufacturers, importers, wholesale and retail dealers, rests still on the same fundamental idea of mutual advantage, and every member of it is, or ought to be, a public benefactor and servant at the same time that he is making gain for himself; so that, so far from being inapplicable here, there is nothing to which this law is more literally and precisely applicable: "Thou shalt love thy neighbor *as* thyself." You shall seek his benefit at the very same time, in the very same transaction, in the very same measure, in which you seek your own. The moment this idea of equivalent is lost sight of and the attempt made to get more than one gives in return, that moment the transaction becomes overreaching, cheating, fraud, swindling, gambling—something, anything, other than fair dealing.

Whatever may be the perils of money-getting, then, it is clear that there is nothing in the essential nature of trade, nothing in a business-life based on sound principles, which should hinder the Christian from entering it with the most generous impulses and the purest ambitions, and pursuing it with the most honorable purpose to serve his generation not only through the profits of his business, but through his business itself. In this spirit men have entered it and continued in it, growing to be larger and nobler Christians all the while. One of the worst things, indeed, about this low view of trade as a kind of legalized freebooting is that it involves so base an injustice to the host of honorable and Christian men in trade, many of whom have not their superiors in point of character in the communities which they adorn.

Only, the Christian in trade must take with him, day by day and hour by hour, as a touchstone by which to try not only his business as a whole, but all the details of its management, this law. He is to try his business as a whole by this test. A legitimate business does not mean the same thing at God's bar that it means in some men's mouths. The question whether any business is legitimate or not resolves itself into the simple question, "Does it, on the whole, benefit society?" "Thou shalt love thy neighbor as thyself" does not mean "Thou shalt pander to his lusts," but "Thou shalt consult his true well-being." It does not give me the right to destroy my neighbor's soul, even if I am willing to destroy my own. It is interpreted for us by the apostle thus: "Let every one of us please his neighbor for his good, to edification."* It is not an adequate justification for a business that it meets a demand. The question is, "Does it meet a need?" It will not satisfy a good conscience in the choice of a calling that "there is money in it" unless there is also public benefit in it. There is a demand for obscene literature; does that justify the writing and the selling of it? There is money in the whisky-traffic; does that justify the distilling and the retailing of that which destroys men's bodies, blasts their homes, ruins their souls and burdens society with an ever-growing army of paupers and criminals? Shall we be told that such a business as that is legitimate? Rather let us say, borrowing one more pungent phrase from Bushnell, that such things as these "are even mockeries of trade in its prime idea, selling what they call goods which they know to be evils."

Is it said that strong drink, for example, has its uses—that it is not necessarily a sin to drink it, and that lives may even be saved by it? Be it so; what then? Let the use be to the abuse as one to one hundred (and that is certainly a generous allowance); shall I blight one hundred homes in the hope of cheering one, shall I imperil one hundred lives in the hope of saving one, and still say that I love my neighbor as myself? Let such a trade be carried on,

* Rom. xv. 2.

if at all, like the trade in poisons, under restrictions and safeguards which will so rigidly curtail the abuses as to turn the balance unquestionably to the side of benefit, or else left altogether alone. There is a deadly sophism in this plea of a possible legitimate use when it is made to justify indiscriminate dealing in that which is known to work an enormous overplus of evil. A man has no more moral right, whatever license the civil government may sell him, to make money at such risk to his neighbors than a resident of a crowded city would have to make money by a powder-mill in his cellar or a slaughter-house in his back yard. So the editor who has one sole criterion of what shall go into his paper—who says, "I am simply a dealer in news and opinions, and my business is to furnish what my customers call for, moral or immoral, pure or impure"—will find out to his cost that he has to reckon with a law which will grind to powder together such moral rubbish and the maker of it.

But this law is a touchstone not only for the choice of a business, but for the conduct of it. Nay, not simply for the conduct of a business, but for the conduct of all those petty transactions in buying and selling, in letting and hiring, in employing and laboring, of which so large a part of the daily life of every one is made up.

"Well, you made a good thing of that," said one to

a friend who told him of a trade in real estate which he had just concluded.—" Yes," was the answer, " and it was as good for the other party as for me;" and added he, " I never feel right about a bargain unless I can say that." "Thou shalt love thy neighbor as thyself" means that, or it means nothing. It means that we should take nothing from our neighbor without the purpose to render a full equivalent for what we receive. The moment that purpose is lost sight of, that moment our dealings cease to be either Christian or honest.

But who shall be the judge of the equivalent? What is a "fair" price for anything? Is it not just what it will bring? In a sense, yes. My neighbor knows a great deal better than I can know how much he wants what I have to supply. It is right that he should look out for himself in this sense, that he should be his own judge of his side of the bargain, *provided* he has, or may be presumed to have, the ability to judge and the means of judging. But suppose he has not? What should we think of the big boy at school who should take advantage of the inexperience of a little fellow in his first trousers to trade his old hacked pocket-knife of soft iron for the little fellow's brand-new knife of Sheffield steel? And yet what is a great deal of the so-called shrewdness of the commercial world but just that—a deliberate advantage taken of manifest ignorance and inexperience to give much less than an equivalent for what is gained? We shall have to answer by and by in a court where that sort of thing will be called, not shrewdness, but stealing.

Nor can I, if I love my neighbor as myself, withhold from him the means of judging what is for his interest. My motive for doing that, if I do it, must certainly be to pass off upon him, under cover of a false impression, less than an equivalent for what I obtain from him. There is another name for that, too, in the court to which we are bound. Such suppression of material knowledge is there known as cheating. "A false balance is abomination to the Lord."* Why? Because it is a contrivance for making the buyer think he is getting what he is not. There is many a man whose weights and measures are up to the strict legal standard, who has expedients much more subtle and quite as effectual for the same end. Does their subtlety lessen the abomination in God's sight? What shall we say, for instance, of the innumerable adulterations by which the commodities we buy, the food we eat, the medicines, even, by which we seek to preserve life, are lowered in value, if not made absolutely harmful? Are they not all expedients to get something for nothing? If a man pays

* Prov. xi. 1.

for a pound of sugar and receives fifteen ounces of sugar and one ounce of sand, he has been robbed of the price of one ounce of sugar. "But," says the dealer, "I made the price just one-sixteenth less than pure sugar would have cost." Still, that does not help the matter, unless the customer knew that his sugar was cheap because it was impure; otherwise, his money has been obtained under a false pretence. He has been in effect lied to in order that he might be robbed.

And what, in the light of this principle of equivalent rendered, shall we say of the various concealments that are practiced of facts material to the question of value? When the director of a railway whose stock commands a high premium, knowing that the road has lost heavily and that its stock must soon decline, "unloads" upon some one whom he knows not to be in possession of these facts, what is this but a scheme for getting more than he gives? How does it differ in principle from the false balance which is abomination to the Lord?

Many years ago, before the days of telegraphs, the Southern mail was once detained two hours at Paulus' Hook to enable certain speculators to reach Philadelphia and make their purchases before its arrival—in other words, to enable them to take advantage of the known ignorance of Philadelphia merchants to drive a bargain to their disadvantage. It may seem a hard thing to say, but it is true for all that, that the spirit which animates all such transactions is the very same which impels the burglar who breaks into a house at night—the desire to wrest from another against his will that for which he gets no return. It was not a minister unversed in the ways of the world, but a lawyer and an authority on the subject of contracts— the French judge Pothier—who laid down this broad rule: "Any deviation from the most exact and scrupulous sincerity is repugnant to the good faith that ought to prevail in contracts. Any dissimulation concerning the subject-matter of the contract and what the opposite party has an interest in knowing is contrary to that good faith."

So far we have assumed that dealings were free on both sides. The case is different where one of the parties is not free, but is forced to buy or sell. Yet here, too, the same Christian law of trade applies, though its application is sometimes less easy. Extortion of every kind, grinding monopolies (when they *are* grinding), "corners" that make dear the necessaries of life and fleece their unsuspecting victims to the bone,—all are condemned by this test. At no time, indeed, does the contrast between grasping selfishness and Christian love of one's neighbor shine out more clearly than when circumstances have delivered one's neighbor into his hands and put it in his power to make his own terms with him. Happy is that man of whom it can be said, as it was said of the late Amos Lawrence, "He was a living example of a successful merchant who had from the earliest period of his business career risen above all artifice, and *had never been willing to turn to his own advantage the ignorance or misfortune of others.*"

"Yes," says one, "that is all very fine. The principle is sound enough, but I could never succeed so in my business. Competition would ruin me." Let him fail, then, if he cannot succeed. If the choice lies between failing in business and failing in character, better a thousand times fail in business. But it is false. He can succeed. To one who complains of the pressure of competition the reply is always in order which Mr. Webster made to the young man who feared that the profession of law was overcrowded: "There is always room at the top." Let a man make himself the best in his calling, and the world will find it out. Men will go in the end where they get their money's worth. There are no tricks of the trade that are a match for *thoroughness*. Those can succeed on the same high plane of integrity on which Lawrence succeeded who will seek success with Lawrence's industry, frugality, perseverance, and application. It is a wretched excuse for the unworthy expedients by which men seek to retrieve the consequences of their own indolence and carelessness to say, "They all do it." It is false; they do not all do it, and no one need do it.

"Oh, but," says another, "such success is slow." Yes, it is slow. But has not God himself warned against the haste to be rich? Have we not already found that the slow road is here the only sure road, and, what is more, the only safe road and the only happy road?

"But then how am I to live up to such a law of trade in my dealings, when those with whom I have to deal are continually plotting to overreach me? What is this but to offer myself as a prey to the rapacity of the unscrupulous, a lamb in the midst of wolves?" And who, then, was it that said, "Behold, I send you forth as sheep in the midst of wolves. Be ye therefore wise as serpents, and harmless as doves"?* Truly, if one cannot take the risks of obedience to God's law, if one thinks sin is safer in this world than righteousness and the devil a surer protector and a better paymaster than the Lord, to such a one there is not much to be said.

But it is urged, again, "This rule is difficult of application." What does it require in this case or in that? Strange what casuists men become, and what perplexing problems they can invent, when their interest lies in evading some plain principle of morals! Granted.

* Matt. x. 16.

It is difficult to apply many times. What then? It will not be too difficult for God to apply when he summons us to an account of our stewardship. And is it not prudence for us to anticipate that testing by squaring our own life at whatever pains to that rule now? The shipbuilder is not wise who waits for the sea to find the holes in his keel; the engineer is not wise who waits for the loaded train to find the flaws in his bridge-cables; yet theirs is but a harmless folly compared with that of him who waits for the day of judgment to expose the hollowness and falsehood of the principles on which he has based his life.

Some years ago a certain Mr. S., being desirous of obtaining a loan, applied to a friend of his—an old and prudent German—to endorse his note, assuring him it would be promptly paid at maturity, and that he should be caused no uneasiness on account of it. The German accepted the statement without distrust, and signed his name. The note soon passed into other hands; but when it became due, the original maker was either too poor or too dishonest to pay it. Great was the consequent surprise of the German at discovering that the endorsement of the note was something beyond the empty form he had supposed, and that Mr. B., the innocent holder into whose hands the note had passed, expected him to pay a sum which he had never intended to pay, and for which he had received no equivalent. Reluctant to part with his hard-earned capital, and indignant at the deceit practiced upon him, he at once sought counsel of an eminent lawyer, in whose hands he placed his cause, determined to resist the collection of the note to the utmost. Judge —— promised to investigate the case, and bade his client call again in a few days. Returning at the appointed time, he was met with the assurance in the most cheerful tone, "My good sir, this note is worthless. You cannot be compelled to pay it." And the lawyer went on to show that for lack of some technicality demanded by the law of the State the promise was not worth the paper it was written on. The German's face lighted up: "What is that you say? I shall not have to pay the note?"—"No."—"And S.? He will not pay it?"—"No."—"And Mr. B.? He will not get his money?"—"No; the note is legally void." For a moment a look of triumph could be read on the German's wrinkled features, but it was instantly succeeded by a more sober expression, "You say Mr. B. will not get his money?"—"No," repeated his counsel.—"Then I will pay the note. *I must die some time.*"

"I must die some time"! Would to God it were written over every desk in the counting-room, over every page of the ledger, on the face of every draft and across every bill: "I must die some time." What a new world it would make if in all our buying and selling, in all our borrowing and lending, in all the relations of this most complicated thing that we call "trade" in which all of us are in some way involved, our hearts might hourly admonish us: "I must die some time"!

V.

COVETOUSNESS AND RETRIBUTION.

V.

Covetousness and Retribution.

THERE is no other one sin against which Jesus so often warned men as the sin of covetousness. Ever and anon through all his teaching these warnings break upon the ear with a solemn monotony, like the deep tones of a fog-bell warning mariners off some dangerous reef. From the frequency and emphasis of these warnings, it is clear that the Master regarded this sin as one of the most formidable obstacles to the salvation of men.

Sometimes these warnings, impressive in themselves, become doubly so from the circumstances under which they were uttered. Thus on one occasion Jesus had been dealing with the most solemn truths that can engage the attention of men—judgment to come and eternal retribution—when suddenly, with the freedom which characterized those informal gatherings, one of the company broke in upon the discourse, apparently before it was concluded, with the singularly inopportune request, "Master, speak to my brother, that he divide the inheritance with me."* The request was suggested, indeed, by the discourse, but suggested in a way that revealed, as hardly anything else would have revealed, the sordid and groveling spirit of the petitioner. Jesus had portrayed a judgment to come. It suggested to this man that judgment was what he would have. Jesus had figured himself as exercising an august authority in that coming judgment. It struck this earthly-minded listener that one who claimed such authority might do something to right the private wrong which rankled in his breast, and which, perhaps, the courts had refused to settle to his mind. So entirely had the things of this world taken possession of him, that even the words of One who spake as never man spake could not lift him above them. So completely had the love of money blinded his spiritual vision, that even when the Son of man was placing before him

> "in dread array
> The pomp of that tremendous day
> When he with clouds should come,"

the man could think of nothing higher than his lawsuits and his losses, and, though dimly conscious, as it would seem, that he was in the presence of a Being

* Luke xii. 13.

of superhuman power and authority, could think of no greater boon to ask of such a Being than that he would put him in possession of a few acres or a few talents of which he thought himself wrongfully dispossessed.

Ministers are occasionally charged with preaching over the heads of their hearers, and sometimes they are made painfully aware that the charge is but too true. In such cases it may be some comfort to remember that here was at least one hearer over whose head Jesus preached; and yet the trouble was not that the preaching was too high, but that the head was too low. All spiritual truth must needs go over the head of him whose mind never rises higher than his farm and his merchandise.

Yet if for the preacher of truth there is comfort in this incident, there is instruction too. For no sooner did this interruption show the Master where this man stood than he at once came down to his level, and, when he had put aside with an almost scornful negative the petty surrogate's dignity in which his petitioner would have installed him, he began at once a new discourse aimed straight the man, with all hearers like-minded, on his own darling theme of money, first smiting his conscience with a warning sharp enough, it should seem, to catch the deafest ear, "Take heed, and beware of covetousness," following it up with a parable pointed enough to pierce the dullest mind—the parable of the Rich Fool.

These tactics of divine wisdom are not yet obsolete, nor is this reiterated warning of divine love to-day unreasonable.

In former chapters attention has been called to the temptation that lurks in the desire of riches, and with tenfold energy and peril in the haste to be rich. We have now to advance a step beyond temptation, and deal with two yet more solemn thoughts—*sin* and *retribution*.

Some reader has said to himself, it may be, as we have surveyed the temptations connected with the desire of riches, "Oh, if that is all, I do not care. I will take the risks." If any one has been disposed to say that, the probabilities are that such a one has already yielded to temptation and is involved in the *sin* of covetousness, which will bring its sure retributions after it.

Two Greek words are commonly used in the New Testament to express on slightly different sides the lust of gain. The rendering of one, "covetousness," conveys to an English reader a suggestion of ambiguity which is absent from the original. The English word carries our mind at once to the tenth commandment, and leads to a confounding of the thing we are here warned against with the sin there forbidden—the unlawful desire of that which is our neighbor's. But neither in Greek nor in Hebrew is there any verbal kinship between the *coveting* of the commandment and the *covetousness* of the New Testament. This latter is, literally, "more-having"—*i. e.*, desire for more (either more than others or more than enough)—and answers precisely to the Old Testament "greed of gain." The other word, though rightly rendered "the love of money," is in the original one word, "money-love," conveying, like the former, the suggestion of something undue or excessive. We might render it by our word "avarice;" and there is about the same difference in shading between the two Greek words as between the two English words—a difference which has been tersely expressed by saying that "avarice keeps what covetousness has gained." But the same warnings apply to both. It is the passion for gain in either form and in all its forms, whether associated with careful hoarding or with lavish spending, against which the word of God so often and so urgently admonishes.

The urgency of these warnings is grounded on three things—the guilt of this passion, its subtlety, and its deadliness.

On its *guilt*. Covetousness is a venial sin in human eyes. It sends no man to prison; it does not even shut a man out of good society, nor always out of the Church. It is not adjudged inconsistent with the highest respectability—hardly inconsistent, in its more refined forms, with the reputation of sanctity. Bishop Wordsworth has well said that the covetousness of the Pharisees "did not disqualify them for exercising a commanding influence, and for being, in the popular mind, patterns of sanctity and objects of general admiration." And to this day the popular standard of judgment is much the same. Many a man stands fair with his fellows, and is even looked up to as a pillar of the church, though he is known to be both grasping and penurious. Men say, "Yes, it is a pity he is so absorbed in business and does not give more liberally; but then he is honest and upright—in fact, a Christian gentleman." How different is God's judgment, as expressed by his apostle in the Epistle to the Ephesians! "For this ye know, that no whoremonger, nor unclean person, nor covetous man, who is an idolater, hath any inheritance in the kingdom of Christ and of God;"* and again in his first letter to the Corinthians: "Be not deceived; neither fornicators, nor idolaters, nor adulterers, nor effeminate, nor abusers of themselves with mankind, nor thieves, nor covetous, nor drunkards, nor revilers, nor extortioners, shall inherit the kingdom of God."† I do not think of any other particular in which the moral standard of the New Testament is in such sharp contrast with the

* Eph. v. 5. † 1 Cor. vi. 9, 10.

current standards of popular judgment as in this classing of covetousness, an excessive love of money—and that not once or twice, but repeatedly, almost uniformly, from beginning to end of the book—with such coarse and vulgar sins as theft, drunkenness, idolatry, and vices which one blushes even to name. Verily, either God's word is altogether wrong on this subject, or else the world's judgment is totally, dangerously wrong.

Between these two we cannot hesitate. The justification of that sterner judgment lies in that suggestive phrase, "Covetousness, which is idolatry."* The covetous man loves money better than he loves God. He dethrones Jehovah and sets up riches, luxury, social influence, or some one of the many things which are in the power of money, in his place. This is his supreme good. This is what he loves with all his heart. To this he looks for blessing; toward this he shapes his life. This is the essence of covetousness. Covetousness is defined as an inordinate desire of gain. Is it asked, What is "inordinate"? Where shall the line be drawn? This is his answer: That is inordinate which puts riches in the first place, which seeks riches first, instead of seeking first the kingdom of God and his righteousness. To do that may not shut a man out of good society, but it will shut him out of the kingdom

* Col. iii. 5.

of God; it may not send him to prison, but it will send him to hell.

But this is a thing difficult to test; and the difficulty of testing it gives to this snare a peculiar *subtlety* which is an added reason for taking heed. Many a reader stumbles at that saying, "The love of money is a root of all kinds of evil,"* and asks himself, What, then? Shall we hate money? Since money is a good thing, even a necessary thing, in its place, why should we not love it within proper bounds? Within proper bounds, doubtless. There is a contempt of money which is as truly an evil as the undue love of it. The wise father finds it necessary to teach his son a just appreciation of the value of money as a point of wholesome training, the neglect of which might prove a lifelong injury. The trouble comes from the unavoidable substitution of the neutral phrase "the love of money" for the Greek word "money-love," which carries with it, like our "greed of gain," its own suggestion of excess. But excess is always a hard thing to measure. The point at which a just appreciation of the value of money passes over into an undue love or worship of it is not easy to fix. And so it comes to pass that covetousness is just one of the sins of which men are least conscious. No man is disposed to believe that he himself loves money too well or

* 1 Tim. vi. 10. (R. V.)

COVETOUSNESS AND RETRIBUTION. 93

pursues riches too eagerly. A Catholic priest who all his life had been hearing confessions is reported to have said that he received confessions of every sin but covetousness; no one had ever confessed that. It is the common experience of ministers that the most earnest sermons on this subject glide right over those who need them the most without producing the slightest impression—are perhaps even applauded afterward without the least suspicion that they had a personal application. Nothing short of Nathan's "Thou art the man,"* ever reaches such hearers; even that is more likely to be resented as a slander and an insult than accepted as a convicting judgment.

The difficulty of recognizing this sin in one's self is increased by its progressive character. One starts, it may be, from a moderate and proper appreciation of the value of money, but in his pursuit of it the passion for it grows till it becomes an absorbing worship, without his ever knowing that there has been any change.

But unconsciousness of the sin makes no difference with the *deadliness of the retributions* which it draws after it. "Which some reaching after have been led astray from the faith and pierced themselves through with many sorrows." † What a picture of a ruined life—ruined for time and for eternity! And all by

* 2 Sam. xii. 7. † 1 Tim. vi. 10 (R. V.)

this respectable sin, this half-unconscious sin of covetousness!

The heaviest part of this retribution is, of course, future, but not all. It is ordained, in the government of God, that our vices should be our scourges, that they should work out in part their own retribution, and that here. To this, covetousness is no exception. It is a bold figure which the apostle James makes use of when he pictures the very treasures of the rich, heaped up by oppression, as becoming the sources of their torment: "Your gold and silver is cankered; and the rust of them shall be a witness against you, and shall eat your flesh as it were fire."* But it suggests a startling truth. Look, then, with me at some of these earthly retributions of covetousness. They do not all come, nor in the same degree, upon all. They are not all connected with the same forms of the lust of gain. But some of them will come to every man who turns from seeking first the kingdom of God and his righteousness to chase the glittering bubble of riches.

The first of these retributions is negative. It is simple disappointment. But what a disappointment! "He that loveth silver shall not be satisfied with silver, nor he that loveth abundance with increase." † "Take heed, and beware of covetousness; for a man's

---

* James v. 3. † Eccl. v. 10.

life consisteth not in the abundance of the things which he possesseth."* The emphasis here is on the word "abundance." There is where the covetous man makes his mistake. This is the lie with which the devil lures him on. The devil always allures with a lie. All our lusts are, as the apostle calls them, "deceitful lusts." † They are "juggling fiends,"

> "That palter with us in a double sense;
> That keep the word of promise to our ear,
> And break it to our hope."

So is it with this lust of gain. Money lures its dupe onward with the display of its power, only to mock him at last with the discovery of its weakness. He is like the child grasping after the motes in the sunbeam. He closes his hand upon them, opens it again, and, lo! there is nothing there! The motes are there, perhaps, but the light which glorified them he could not hold; and without it they are worthless, they are not even visible. Yet he is not undeceived. He still thinks the trouble to be that he has not enough, and so he grasps after more, and yet more, with the same invariable result. The thirst of his soul is never quenched. For the truth is, these things have no power to quench it. He needs not more, but something *else*. A man's life consisteth not at all in the things which

* Luke xii. 15. † Eph. iv. 22.

he possesseth; no, not even in the utmost conceivable abundance of them. The ancients taught this lesson with great power in their fable of Midas almost perishing of starvation through the very answer to his prayer that everything he touched might turn to gold. Few sights in life are more pathetic than the sight of a man who has devoted his energies to making money, starving his intellect, repressing his affections, cutting himself off from the enjoyment of social and domestic ties, and from all large sympathy with enterprises of utility and beneficence, sitting at last amidst a magnificence which he has worn himself out in procuring and has no capacity to enjoy, like one who has built up around himself with patient toil a solid wall without an outlet, within which, as in a living tomb, he must starve and die.

Do you know the story of the French miser Foscue? Becoming fearful that the government would discover and tax his secretly accumulated wealth, Foscue dug a vault beneath his cellar, which he closed by a trap-door with a spring lock. In this vault he hid his gold, going down from time to time to add to it or to feast his eyes upon it. At length Foscue disappeared. It was surmised that he had fled the country with his hoards in some disguise. Months passed, and he did not appear. Finally his house was seized and publicly sold. While the buyer's workmen were repairing the building they saw the trap-door, opened the vault, and found the miser's corpse among his money-bags. Candle in hand, he had gone down to the den of his idol, the door with its spring lock had accidentally closed upon him, and he had miserably perished in the midst of his gold. It is not often that a retribution so striking in its poetic justice overtakes the covetous; yet what is this, after all, but a parable of what happens to every man who lives for riches, only to find in his riches the grave of his manhood?

The son of a laboring-man sets out in life as a professing Christian. He obtains a clerkship in a mercantile house, and advances till he becomes a partner in the firm. As riches increase liberality and Christian zeal diminish till his shriveled soul scarce bears a trace of the Master's image. At length he purchases a large estate, builds a costly mansion, and soon after occupying it sickens and dies. Just before his death he exclaims as he looks back over that life of successful failure, "My prosperity has been my ruin!"

Add to this the physical retributions which overtake so many. If there is a slave on earth doomed to drudge under the lash till worn-out nature drops exhausted, it is the devotee of Mammon. What mean this increase of nervous diseases, this alarming advance of the percentage of insanity, these sudden deaths and hopeless break-downs in the prime of life, at which physicians and statisticians shake their heads? Largely, this is the fruit of the haste to be rich. I would not judge uncharitably in this matter. I do not forget how many are driven to these calamities by the pressure of the life about them, the exactions of others, the needs of those dependent on them, or even by high ambitions for usefulness. Nevertheless, I do say that in multitudes of cases the greed of gain is alone responsible. It is not work, but overwork, that breaks men down, and not so much overwork, even, as worry—the worry born of an eager, grasping ambition that cannot be content with a little, but strains every nerve to be rich. And the greater the haste to be rich and the more exciting the expedients to which this haste impels, the greater is the physical strain, and hence the danger of premature collapse. If men would moderate their desires for this world's goods and bend their energies more to the culture of their minds and the training of their souls, they would live longer and more vigorous lives, as well as happier ones. The epitaph on many a strong man dead in his prime, if honestly written, would be, "A sacrifice offered up by his own hand on the altar of Mammon."

Look, again, at the loneliness and friendlessness which are peculiarly the lot of the covetous. There are some sins more or less social in their nature. They do not form a tie of true friendship—sin never does that—

but they lead to companionship. They promote a sort of fellowship. Not so with covetousness. It alienates; it dries up the sympathies of the man himself and repels the affections of others. The name of the covetous man becomes a synonym for selfishness or oppression. If he is successful, his riches but isolate him the more completely; they make him an object of jealousy and dislike. Indeed, this is the tendency of riches, quite apart from any covetous spirit back of them. Riches are a social barrier hard to pass over, and that quite as much from jealousy in the poor as from pride in the rich; and for that very reason they are a barrier which only the most genuine simplicity and benevolence on the part of their possessors can overcome. If, instead of this, they are amassed or hoarded in a covetous spirit, their possession is embittered by the consciousness that they have ensured to their possessor the envy and ill-will of the great mass of his fellowmen. But we have not taken the full measure of the retributions which wait upon covetousness even in this world till we have traced its offspring, distant by a second remove—till, in other words, we have added to those which spring directly from the indulgence of this passion those which attend upon the hideous brood of frauds, forgeries, embezzlements, perjuries and other crimes of which it is the parent. Would we know how bitter these may be? No need to go beyond the word of God, with its many-sided pictures of human life, to learn the lesson. We may read it in the story of Achan casting covetous eyes upon the spoils which Jehovah had doomed to destruction, and stoned to death for his trespass; in the story of Gehazi, roused to uncontrollable cupidity by the display of Naaman's treasures, and going out from the presence of the prophet a leper as white as snow; above all, in the story of Judas, casting down in the temple the thirty pieces of silver for the sake of which he had been willing to sell his Master, and going out to hang himself. Ah! that story tells us what we cannot afford ever to forget—that the outward penalty is not the only nor the greatest sorrow with which such sinners pierce themselves through. When one of the respectable criminals of our own day, who came to grief by using the money of others as his own, was convicted and sentenced to the penitentiary, he is said to have remarked that that was nothing at all: he had suffered all the torments of the damned already, and this could add nothing to his punishment. What must be the pains of remorse with which that man is racked to whom the disgrace of the convict's garb has become a mere pin-prick too trifling to be felt?

Nor must it be forgotten that all these retributions are multiplied and edged with new bitterness through the family relations. It is the ordering of God that sin should bring its retribution not only upon the sinner himself, but upon all who are bound to him. The Holy Spirit has deemed this law worthy of special emphasis in the case of the covetous: "He that is greedy of gain troubleth his own house."* What it now concerns us to note is that the trouble which through his greed he brings in so many ways upon his house recoils upon his own head as an added curse.

There is a peculiar fitness in this, too, inasmuch as the necessities of one's family are the most frequent and plausible plea in defence of the too eager pursuit of gain. But he who thus makes his family a pretext for his sin will find that in one way or another his family will sooner or later become the avengers of his sin. The father, for example, who has made himself, through absorption in money-getting, a stranger to his own household, and has taught his children to regard the word "father," not as a synonym for "friend, counselor and guide," but simply as a synonym for "purser," need not be surprised to find himself looked upon at last by the children for whom he has toiled, but whose characters he has left untrained, as a mere obstruction to the full possession of the wealth he has amassed for them, and constrained to cry out, with Lear, in the bitterness of his soul,

* Prov. xv. 27.

"How sharper than a serpent's tooth it is
To have a thankless child!"

Or when, in the mad haste to be rich, one has strained the pliant nerves until they have snapped, and is tossed aside a shattered wreck, it may be the bitterest part of his punishment to find himself a useless burden upon loving hands to which he should have been a strong support. Or, like Gilman, the forger, he may find the bitterest drop in his cup of sorrows to be the breaking heart and reeling brain of a wife who would gladly have braved poverty with him had he been frank with her, but whom, with a cowardly selfishness which he mistook for kindness, he had chosen rather to keep in ignorance and maintain in luxury at the expense of others.

There is a heartbreaking anguish in these words from the published confession of a defaulter to the directors of the bank which he had plundered: "O my God! What will my wife and children do? Be kind to them. . . . I must be dead to them. O my God! I do love them, and this is worse than death. And now, a lone, disgraced man, I go out into some strange place to begin again, with all I love behind me and out of my reach. . . . Be kind and merciful to them. Let me work. Give me a chance to help them."

"Pierced through with many sorrows"! Ah, verily! Yet all these are but the beginning of sorrows. If such the beginning, what shall the end be—that end foreshadowed in the question of Jesus, "What shall it profit a man, if he shall gain the whole world and lose his own soul?"* "For this ye know of a surety, that no ... covetous man ... hath any inheritance in the kingdom of Christ and God. Let no man deceive you with empty words" (let none try to explain away these stern threatenings of God's word); "for because of these things cometh the wrath of God upon the sons of disobedience."†

Have you ever reflected, my reader—you who think with the world that covetousness is a little fault, a failing which even leans to virtue's side—upon that parable of the Rich Man and Lazarus? What sent that rich man to that tormenting flame? What parched that tongue that pleaded in vain for so much as one cooling drop? Not his riches; Father Abraham, too, had been rich. Not dishonesty; there is no hint that his were ill-gotten gains. It was simply that he loved riches better than he loved the service of God and the good of his fellow-man. There is no sin brought to his charge in the parable but covetousness. Yet he died and was buried, "and in hell he lifted up his eyes, being in torments."‡

"*Take heed and beware of covetousness.*"

* Mark viii. 36. † Eph. v. 5, 6 (R. V.).
‡ Luke xvi. 23.

The more one studies the Saviour's teachings, the more clearly is it seen that He who knew what was in man regarded covetousness as the destroyer of more souls in his time than any other one thing. Would he reach, think you, any other conclusion were he to come to Christian America to-day?

VI.

MONEY AS A TEST OF CHARACTER.

VI.
Money as a Test of Character.

"CHILON would say," says Lord Bacon in his Apophthegms, "'Gold is tried with a touchstone, and men are tried with gold.'" What a pity to be reminded, as we read, that Bacon himself, with all his gifts, with all his services to the world, tried by that touchstone, was proved to be but base metal, and left a sullied memory to be handed down in Pope's biting epigram,

"The wisest, brightest, meanest of mankind."

Our Lord himself illustrated the method of applying this touchstone in the case of the young man who came to him asking, "Good Master, what shall I do that I may inherit eternal life?"* Jesus tried him in various ways. He applied, one after another, the commandments of the second table, and the young man bore all without flinching. In his own judg-

* Mark x. 17.

ment, at least, he was equal to all these tests. Then Jesus applied the money-test, "Go thy way, sell whatsoever thou hast and give to the poor, and thou shalt have treasure in heaven,"* and straightway the weakness of the young man's character was revealed. He was not capable of self-denial. The earthly was more to him than the heavenly. So he went away sorrowful, too surely conscious that he had been weighed in the balances and found wanting.

That was one way of applying this touchstone to character, but the ways are innumerable. Indeed, I do not know that there is any other one thing which, from the very nature of the case, is so variously and universally applicable a test of character as this. This because of its representative character. Money stands for so many things, it serves so many uses, it represents so wide a range of possibilities, that there is no man, prince or peasant, merchant or minister, but is put to the proof by it in one way or another. From our first glimpse of the glittering bait, through all our getting and handling and spending and losing of it, down to our final parting with it at the grave's edge, it is the occasion of a perpetual and manifold self-revelation. We are tested by the proffer of it, tested still more thoroughly by its possession, tested in some respects most severely of all by its loss.

* Mark x. 21.

We are tested by the proffer of it. This was one of the tests by which the Son of man himself was tried; for when the devil took him up into a high mountain, and, showing him all the kingdoms of the world and the glory of them, said, "All these things will I give thee, if thou wilt fall down and worship me,"* what was this but the offer of a colossal bribe, of riches more stupendous than were ever offered to man before or since—the sum-total, in fact, of all that money can procure—as the price of a single act of disloyalty to the Father whose will he had come to do? What a contrast between the triumphant bearing of that test and the lamentable failure of Judas in the presence of the thirty pieces of silver of the chief priests!

One will say, perhaps, that a money-bribe is but a coarse test of character. Yet Judas's character was so fair that even the disciples who were his daily companions were deceived by it till that test disclosed its hollowness. Ananias and Sapphira passed even with the apostles for worthy disciples of the Lord Jesus till the money-test revealed their selfishness and insincerity. The world is full of just such characters—characters which seem strong and sound, yet give way under the strain of an opportunity to make money; so full of them that the cynic maintains—falsely, thank God!

* Matt. iv. 9.

but with too much show of reason—that every man has his price. Let us but recall the lesson of those sad collapses of reputation to which reference has been made in a former chapter. These were characters which had borne every other test of ordinary life without being suspected of unsoundness, yet proved hollow and rotten by this final test—this coarse test, if you please—of money left in their hands, which was not theirs. A coarse test? Ah! but it is forgotten that money stands for all the delights which imagination pictures and self-indulgence craves. It stands for a magnificent house and charming pleasure-grounds; for the delights of travel, the charm of mountain and sea-side, the marvels of foreign lands; for the choice treasures of art, the privileges of cultivated leisure; for social triumphs or political preferment. To offer men money is to offer them the key to an earthly paradise, to an enchanted bower of delights, which imagination peoples with every charm that can bewilder the sense and intoxicate the soul. Is there not a severe test in the offer of such a key?

Say that in the form of a direct bribe money appeals chiefly to baser natures; there are other modes of applying this test subtler and more searching. There is an old saw which bids us never to account that we know any man till we have divided an inheritance with him. In other words, it warns us that one who has borne successfully the usual tests of every-day life may yet be found wanting in fairness and unselfishness when tried by the opportunity to take more than his share of a sum of money which death has put within his reach. And truly the records of the probate court bring to light strange revelations concerning characters that have passed for irreproachable. The dividing of an inheritance means too often the dividing of a family, because, alas! it brings to light on either side and on all sides an utter lack of that magnanimity which shone out so grandly in old Abraham when he divided with Lot the God-given inheritance of Canaan: "Let there be no strife, I pray thee, between me and thee, and between my herdmen and thy herdmen, for we be brethren. Is not the whole land before thee? Separate thyself, I pray thee, from me. If thou wilt take the left hand, then I will go to the right; or if thou depart to the right hand, then I will go the left."*

Buying and selling is a test of the same sort, in the opportunities it affords to overreach, to get more than one's due. It is no idle jest when men say that he who can be a Christian in a horse-trade can be a Christian anywhere. There is a sound philosophy of human nature in that. It is true that he who, in a transaction in which the opportunity for overreaching

* Gen. xiii. 8, 9.

is ample, can withstand the temptation of unfair gain, approves himself worthy of a large confidence.

In another way Agassiz's famous reply, "I have no time to make money," illustrates the kind of testing we are considering. For some men it is all right to take time to make money: that is the talent which God has intrusted to them, and it is their business to make the most of it in his service. But here was a man who had within him the consciousness of a higher mission. The opportunity to make money came to him as a temptation to renounce that mission and choose a life of luxury and self-indulgence rather than a life of usefulness and loyalty to the inner divine prompting. Think how many have failed under just that test! Think how many high careers have been abandoned, how many noble enterprises have suffered shipwreck, for a chance to make money! Think of all the "lost leaders" of whom it might be sung!—

"Just for a handful of silver he left us,
    Just for a ribbon to stick in his coat—
Found the one gift of which Fortune bereft us,
    Lost all the others she lets us devote.
    *   *   *   *   *   *   *   *
"We shall march prospering, not through his presence;
    Songs may inspirit us, not from his lyre;
Deeds will be done while he boasts his quiescence,
    Still bidding crouch whom the rest bade aspire.

"Blot out his name, then; record one lost soul more,
  One task more declined, one more footpath untrod;
  One more triumph for devils and sorrow for angels,
  One wrong more to man, one more insult to God."

And even among the disciples of Him who, though he was rich, yet for our sakes became poor, how many are the followers of that Demas of whom an apostle sadly wrote, "Demas hath forsaken me, having loved this present world"!*

But the *use* that one makes of his money, once gained, is a test of character even more thorough and comprehensive than his treatment of the opportunity to gain it. This is the central thought in our Lord's parable of the Unjust Steward: "If therefore ye have not been faithful in the unrighteous mammon, who will commit to your trust the true riches." † Tell me how a man spends his money, and I will tell you what the man is. Is he a miser, is he a sensualist, is he controlled by his domestic affections, is the love of display his ruling passion, is he a worshiper of art, is he a philanthropist, a reformer, is his soul on fire with the love of Christ? His cash-book, if only it be truthful and minute enough, will tell the story. Money is simply opportunity, and character is always shown by the use of opportunity. Money is raw material for any fabric, at the pleasure of the

* 2 Tim. iv. 10.   † Luke xvi. 11.

owner. In the things to which he converts it he reveals himself, as the sculptor reveals himself in the shapes he impresses upon the plastic clay. We sometimes test our children at Christmas-time by a present of money in lieu of other gifts, watching to see what they will do with it, and, according as it goes for candy or for books or for tools or to the savings' bank or to the mission-box, we not only forecast their future, but regulate our own subsequent liberality to them, trusting them with more or less as they thus reveal their fitness or unfitness to be trusted. And do we never reflect that this is precisely what our heavenly Father is doing with us—trying us with a little of the unrighteous mammon, that we may show whether we are fit to receive the true riches?

The ampler the opportunity, the more abundant the material, the fuller, of course, is the revelation of character. If money is always a test of character, riches are peculiarly so. All the way from a James Fisk to an Amos Lawrence riches reveal the man. Unhappily, we are constrained to recognize that comparatively few bear the test successfully. Abraham bore it; he stands a noble example for all time of a man whose riches only brought out with greater clearness the lustre of his character. Job bore it; Satan made light of Job's blamelessness in prosperity and professed to treat it as purely mercenary: "Doth Job fear God for naught? Hast thou not made an hedge about him, and about his house, and about all that he hath on every side? Thou hast blessed the work of his hands, and his substance is increased in the land."* But in saying this Satan was really paying a high tribute to the strength of Job's character and the genuineness of his piety. He knew well enough that it is not the natural effect of great riches and uninterrupted prosperity to make men seem more devout and heavenly-minded. He ought to have known, if he did not know, that a character which had borne that test as Job's had borne it was not likely to break down under the test of poverty and adversity. Nor do we need to go back to patriarchal times to find such men. Thank God we have them with us to-day—men who, with incomes which dwarf those of the great majority of the community in which they live, yet preserve in the midst of their wealth a simplicity so unfeigned, a generosity so uncontracted, a heavenly-mindedness so unclouded, that when we see them or call them to mind their money is the last thing we think of.

But these are the exceptions. Some witticisms have been leveled at the phrase, so common in literature, "Poor, but honest," as though it were an absurdity and an injustice to the poor to assume that poverty and honesty were unlikely to go together. There is

* Job i. 9, 10.

some truth in the criticism, and some falsehood. Dishonesty is the peculiar temptation of the poor, as Agur recognized when he prayed, "Lest I be poor and steal, and take the name of my God in vain." But with the same propriety we might speak, on the other hand, of an Abraham or of a Job as "rich, but spiritual." For if dishonesty is the temptation of the poor, worldliness is not less the temptation of the rich—as Agur also recognized when he prayed, "Lest I be full and deny thee, and say, Who is the Lord?"*

Is it not undeniable that but few rich men use their riches as they thought to do before they had them? Then they had splendid visions of the needs they would relieve, the institutions they would endow, the enterprises of philanthropy they would set on foot. But these visions are seldom realized. "I have never seen," says Landor, "great possessions excite to great alacrity. Usually they enfeeble the sympathies, and often overlie and smother them." Partly it is that the character has deteriorated in the process of getting rich—the man is not the same man that he was when poor—but largely it is that character has been tested and found wanting: the man is not the man he thought he was before he was tried. Had the riches come to him suddenly in the very hour of his generous dreams,

---

* Prov. xxx. 9.

he would have borne the test no better—perhaps not so well.

The simple fact, patent to every one, is that the great fortunes of the world are seldom and meagrely available for the great needs of the world—at least, until death wrenches them from reluctant hands. A writer in *The Church Missionary Intelligencer* for 1886, who had been looking up the gifts of the British aristocracy to foreign missions, ascertained that, for the year preceding, the contributions of the titled and wealthy to the treasury of the Church Missionary Society amounted to six thousand five hundred and fifty dollars—a little over a thousand pounds—from three hundred and sixty-two individuals; only seventeen dollars a man from the richest privileged class in the world to the treasury of one of the great missionary agencies of their own nation and Church! What a revelation of character, what a story of self-indulgence, of unfaithful stewardship, of religious indifference, is contained in such figures!

Nor should we overlook the peculiar test of character which is involved in riches by reason of their removal of the ordinary stimulus to exertion. There is nothing ignoble—rather, there is everything honorable—in working for a living. But there is something ignoble in ceasing to work at all when one has not to work for a living. This world is no place for drones.

There are higher motives than mere bread and butter which should impel every man and woman whom God has endowed with the requisite capacity to some useful and well-ordered activity. It is when riches have removed the spur of hunger that we discover how far character is under the sway of these higher motives. Too often the discovery is a sad disappointment. I have in mind a young man, born to great possessions, whose whole life, so far as I know, instead of being devoted to the pursuit of any one of the thousand worthy enterprises in science, in education, in exploration, in philanthropy, which his wealth would have put within his power, has been passed in a really earnest effort to kill time by devotion to yachting, coaching, polo, and other equally empty pursuits.

If there is any calling in life which is presumed to be entered upon from disinterested and unmercenary motives, it is the ministry of the gospel. And yet so severe is the test of riches, and so often does even the minister, falling heir to them, turn his back upon the pulpit, that they are worthy to be held in especial honor who keep right on with their work, though abundantly able to live in idleness. It becomes us to remember, therefore, when we criticise, as most of us are so ready to do, the selfishness and worldliness of the rich, that the difference between them and ourselves may be, far more than we think,

A TEST OF CHARACTER.

simply a difference in thoroughness of testing. Were the same measure of the unrighteous mammon entrusted to us, it is not at all certain that we should prove worthier to receive it or more faithful in our use of it.

Is it certain, indeed, that we do bear any better, relatively, the milder application of the same great test? Exhibitions of selfishness and pride are much less startling on a small scale than on a large one, but they may reveal just as unsound a character. It is natural to point the finger of scorn at the millionaire who contributes a hundred dollars where he should contribute a thousand, forgetting, while we do so, that, in putting a dime upon the plate which should have received our dollar, we have laid ourselves open to equal scorn. The difference between a dime and a dollar looks trifling; the difference between a hundred dollars and a thousand looks great. But they subtend the same arc; they measure the same degree of parsimony.

A pitiable lack of honor has revealed itself before now in so small a matter as a five-cent car-fare, while, on the other hand, it took but two mites, which make a farthing, so to test the character of a certain widow as to win from Him who sat over against the treasury a commendation which lifted her up upon a pinnacle as an example to all generations to come.

Yet another searching test of character comes with the *loss* of money. Few things bring out more clearly the pure gold of true manhood and true piety, or, contrariwise, the lack of them, than a reverse of fortune. Nothing shows more clearly than the way in which men part with money, whether they have made it their servant or their master.

It was easy for Satan to sneer at the unaffected piety of Job in the midst of his riches; but when those riches made to themselves wings and flew away in one black day of disaster, how truly devilish appeared that sneer in the presence of the serene cheerfulness that could say, "The Lord gave, and the Lord hath taken away; blessed be the name of the Lord"!* Doubtless we have all seen men who never seemed to be anything remarkable, or to rise above a commonplace sort of goodness, until some sudden calamity swept away their property; and then we saw with surprise and delight what stuff was in them, what courage, what cheerfulness, what mastery of circumstances, what manly self-respect, what unshaken trust—nay, joy—in the Lord.

It is, then, not a small part of life—it is a very great part of life—to know how to bear ourselves aright in this one matter of money. Of him who can do this—who can renounce money without reluctance, seek

* Job i. 21.

money without greediness and without unfairness, possess money without worldliness and without pride, expend money without wastefulness and without selfishness, lose money without disheartenment and without whining, and part from all his money at last without one lingering regret,—it may be said, in such measure as those words can be spoken of any member of this fallen race, "Mark the perfect man, and behold the upright."* And all this is summed up in one word—*faithfulness*. It is all covered by the one broad conception of stewardship.

God is trying us all by this touchstone to-day—every day—and his testing is never aimless, never wanton. It looks to a great future; it leads up to a solemn award: "If ye have not been faithful in the unrighteous mammon, who will commit to your trust the true riches?" †

"The true riches"! I do not think that Christ meant by that what we may call the riches of the soul, the graces of sanctified character. He was speaking of that reward of responsibility to be put upon those who are proved worthy of it. We cannot tell what these true riches are; we only know that the life of God's saints in eternity is to be still an embodied life, having to do, therefore, with the material creation; that in that life one star will differ from another

* Ps. xxxvii. 37. † Luke xvi. 11.

star in glory; that there will be a vast difference in the responsibilities with which even the saved will be entrusted; and that, whatever those resources are by which the work of eternity is to be done, and which, in contrast with "corruptible things, as silver and gold,"* merit the name of the true riches, they are reserved for those who prove their fitness for them by the success with which they bear the test of the unrighteous mammon, wherewith it is their Master's pleasure first to prove them.

With all earnestness, then, let us seek grace from on high to be faithful in that which is least, that we may be found worthy to receive much; to be faithful in that which is another's, and is but loaned to us for a season, that we may be found worthy to receive that which shall be everlastingly our own.

* 1 Pet. i. 18.

THE END.

www.ingramcontent.com/pod-product-compliance
Lightning Source LLC
Chambersburg PA
CBHW022141160426
43197CB00009B/1385